GOSPEL FAVORITES FOR
CHOIR, ENSEMBLE, OR CONGREGATION

BY JOSEPH LINN

ARRANGED FOR USE IN MEDLEYS OR INDIVIDUALLY

A sequel to *Moving Up to Gloryland*

COMPILED BY KEN BIBLE

KANSAS CITY, MO 64141

Step into the Water

K.T.

KIRK TALLEY
Arr. by Joseph Linn

CHORUS: unison
VERSE 1: 1st half, SATB; 2nd half, unison
CHORUS: SATB
VERSE 2: 1st phrase, men unison; 2nd phrase, ladies unison;
3rd phrase, SATB; 4th phrase, all unison
CHORUS: SATB; coda

13
G
G
Am/G
G
G
G°
G
G°
G
Am/G
G
Step in - to the wa - ter; wade out a lit - tle bit deep - er.
last - Repeat
Extended choral ending: last time to Coda
17
D7
Em
Bm/D
D7
Bm/D
Am7
Bm/D
D7
G
G
Fine
Come join an - gels sing - ing prais - es to the Lamb of God.
Slow - last
22
N.C.
D9
G
G°7
G
Am/G
G
G
G
Am/G
G
Am/G
1. It is time we, the peo - ple, stand up for what is
2. There is vic - t'ry for the Chris - tian who walks the nar - row
26
G
D7
C/D
Am/C
C
right. It is time we squared our shoul - ders back,
way; There has been a prize ap - point - ed for the

29
C7
C/G
G
N.C.
D9
G
G°7
raised our swords to fight. For the Bi - ble is our
soul who does not stray. Oh, I want to live for
32
G
Am/G
G
B
Bsus/C♯
B7/D♯
Em
wea - pon and the Spir - it is our shield. The
Je - sus, be all that I should be, So that
CD 1:2
1st time
CD 1:3
2nd time
35
Am
Am7
Bm/D
D7
Am/D
Bm/D
Am7
Bm/D
Am/D
Church needs more of its mem - bers to be work - ers in the
I can rest with Him for - ev - er, live e - ter - nal -
38
1
2 Song Ending
D.S. al Fine
2 Extended Choral Ending
D.S. al Coda
G
G
G
G
G
G
field.
ly.
ly.

CODA
44
God.
CODA
G
G
G
G
48
D7
Em
Bm/D
D7
Am/C
Bm
Am7
D7/A
C/D
D7
Come join an - gels sing - ing prais - es to the Lamb of
52
G
G
G
G
G
G
Am/G
G
God. Step in - to the wa - ter.

FARTHER ALONG Medley

Arr. by Joseph Linn

FARTHER ALONG
VERSE 1: SAT
CHORUS: SATB
VERSE 4: SAT
CHORUS: SATB; medley ending

THE UNCLOUDED DAY
VERSE 1: unison
CHORUS: SATB
VERSE 3: SATB (basses sing melody)
CHORUS: SATB; medley ending

Farther Along

Rev. W.B.S. Rev. W. B. STEVENS

be thus all the day long, While there are oth-ers liv-ing a-bout us, nev-er mo-lest-ed tho' in the wrong.
home so lone-ly and drear. Then do we won-der why oth-ers pros-per, liv-ing so wick-ed year af-ter year.
days to la-bor and wait." Toils of the road will then seem as noth-ing as we sweep through the beau-ti-ful gate.
from His home in the sky, Then we shall meet Him in that bright man-sion; We'll un-der-stand it all by and by.
(1) all the day long,
CHORUS
Far-ther a-long we'll know all a-bout it; Far-ther a-long we'll un-der-stand why. Cheer up, my broth-er, live in the sun-shine; We'll un-der-
why, un-der-stand why.

CD 1:5
1st time
20
E♭ Cm7 Fm Fm9 B♭7
stand it all by and
1-3
E♭ A♭ E♭
by.
by, all by and by.
4 Song Ending
E♭ A♭ E♭
by.
by, all by and by.
4 Medley Ending
23
E♭ A♭/E♭ A♭add9/E♭ E♭ E♭
by, by and by.
4 Medley Ending
23
CD 1:6
26
F F

The Unclouded Day

J.K.A.

J. K. ALWOOD

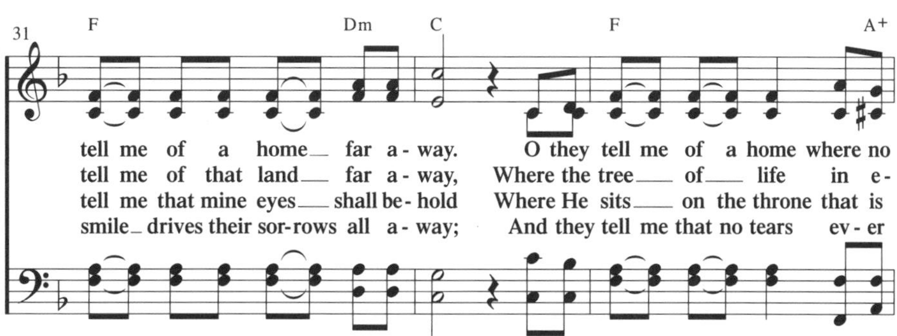

CHORUS
38
F
B♭
F
F
F
C
F
F
B♭
F
F
F
C
Gm
C
F
F
A
O the land of cloud-less day! O the land of an un-cloud-ed
42
C
F
A+
B♭
B♭
D
F
day! O they tell me of a home where no storm-clouds rise;
CD 1:7
1st time
45
F
B♭
F
F
F
A
B♭6
F
C
C7
1-3
F
4 Song Ending
F
O they tell me of an un - cloud-ed day. day.
4 Medley Ending
49
F
F
B♭
F
F
F
A
B♭6
rit.
F
C
C7
F
day. O they tell me of an un - cloud-ed day.
End of Medley

Champion of Love

P.C. and C.C.

PHIL and CAROLYN CROSS
Arr. by Joseph Linn

VERSE 1: solo
CHORUS: SATB
VERSE 2: 1st phrase, men unison;
remainder of verse, all unison
CHORUS: SATB; extended choral ending
CHORUS: unison through "...pow'r away.";
remainder of chorus, SATB; 3rd ending

12

C/G Cadd9/G D/F♯ D/E D D6 C

white. His height ex-ceeds the heav-ens; His weight out-weighs the world; His
down. But I will nev-er count Him out, For I'm a wit-ness of the

15

D D6 C Cadd9/E D7sus D7

reach reach-es ev-'ry-where; His age is ev-er-more.
day He rose to re-tain the ti-tle– "Champ-pi-on of Love".

CHORUS

18

Bm D7/A G Bm7 Cadd9 D7

He is high-er than the high-est, great-er than the great; No

21

G Am/G G Am/E G/D Gadd9/B C G/B Am7

one will ev-er take His pow'r a-way. He's more might-y than the

25

D C/D G G/B C C

might-i-est; He reigns from a-bove. He's the
a-bove, a-bove.

CD 1:10
2nd time
29
G
1
A9
D
C/D
Bm/D
D7
all - time, un - dis - put - ed, un - de - feat - ed Cham - pi - on of
31
CD 1:9
Love.
31
G
Gsus
G
C/G
2 Song Ending
35
A9
D
C/D
Bm/D
D7
G
G
un - de - feat - ed Cham - pi - on of Love.

2 Extended Choral Ending
D.S.
38
A9
D
C/D
Bm/D
D7
G
un - de - feat - ed Cham - pi - on of Love.
3 (Continuation of extended choral ending)
40
A9
D
C/D
Bm/D
D7
G
un - de - feat - ed Cham - pi - on, the all - time, un - dis - put - ed,
42
A9
D
C/D
Bm/D
D7
G
un - de - feat - ed Cham - pi - on, the all - time, un - dis - put - ed
44
A/G
Gm7
Gsus/D
G
(8)
Cham - pi - on, the Cham - pi - on of Love.

ON MY JOURNEY Medley

Arr. by Joseph Linn

IT'S ALRIGHT NOW
VERSE 1: SATB
CHORUS: SATB
VERSE 3: ladies unison through "...nearing home.";
remainder of verse, SATB
CHORUS: SATB; medley ending

I WOULDN'T TAKE NOTHIN' FOR MY JOURNEY NOW
CHORUS: SATB
VERSE 1: 1st half, unison; 2nd half, SATB
CHORUS: SATB; coda

It's Alright Now

M.L. MOSIE LISTER

10
G
Dsus/A
G/B
C
G/D
D7
G
C/G
G
Je-sus took my load;
drew me to His side.
soul is near-ing home.
It's al-right now– I'm His, I know.
It's al-right now, for I'm His own.
It's al-right now– I'm heav-en-bound.
It's al-right now,
CHORUS
13
N.C.
G
C
G
It's al-right now, for I am in my Sav-ior's care.
It's al-right now, for I am in my Sav-ior's care. It's al-right
16
D7
D7/F♯
C/E
D7
G
It's al-right now, my Sav-ior hears and an-swers prayer.
now, my Sav-ior hears and an-swers prayer. He'll walk with
18
C
G
Gsus/A
G/B
D7
G
He'll walk be-side me 'til I climb the heav'n-ly stair,
me 'til I climb the heav'n-ly stair, And ev-'ry-

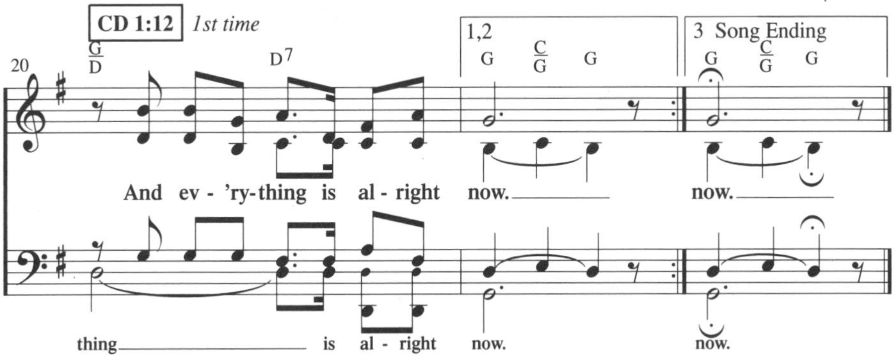

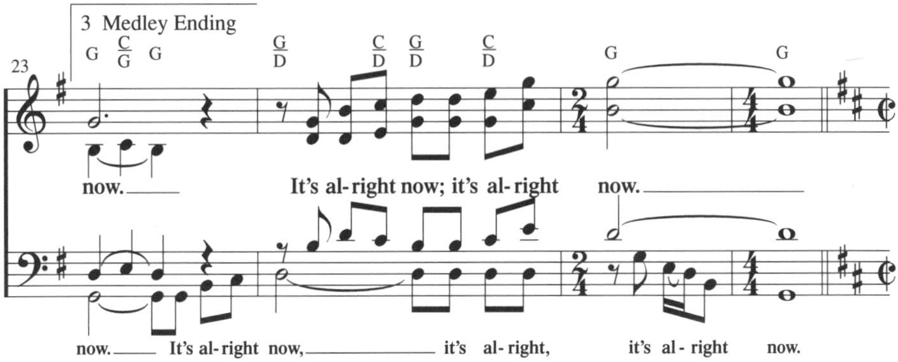

CD 1:12 1st time
1,2
3 Song Ending
G/D D7 G C/G G G C/G G
20
And ev - 'ry-thing is al - right now. now.
thing is al - right now. now.

3 Medley Ending
G C/G G G/D C/D G/D C/D G G
23
now. It's al-right now; it's al-right now.
now. It's al-right now, it's al-right, it's al-right now.

I Wouldn't Take Nothin' for My Journey Now

C.G. and J.D.

CHARLES (RUSTY) GOODMAN and JIMMIE DAVIS

27
Em7 F♯m/A A13 D N.C. N.C.
CD 1:13

CHORUS
31
D/F♯ D/A D D
Well, I would-n't take noth - in' for my jour - ney now;

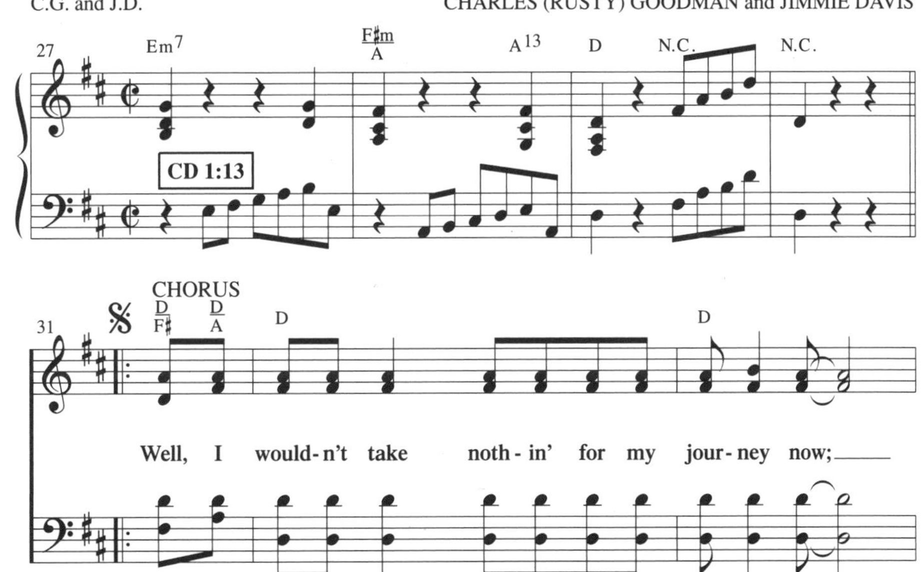

34
G
G
D
I've got to make it to heav-en some- how, Tho' the dev- il tempts me and
37
D
D/A
A
A
A7/C♯
D
tries to turn me a - round. He's of-fered ev- 'ry-thing that's
41
D
D7
Gadd9
G
Gadd9
G
Gadd9
got a name– All the wealth I want and world - ly fame. If I
Medley: last time to Coda
44
D/A
A7
G/A
A7
D
G/D
D
Fine
could, still I would-n't take noth-in' for my jour-ney now.

48
D D A7
1. There's noth-in' in the world that-'ll ev - er take the place of God's
2. I start-ed out trav-'lin' for the Lord man-y years a -
51
D D D
love; Sil - ver and gold could nev - er
go; I've had a lot of heart - ache,
54
A7 D D7 D7/F♯
buy His love from a - bove. When my
met a lot of grief and woe. And
57
G G
soul needs heal - in' and I be - gin to feel - in' His
when I would stum - ble, then I would hum - ble

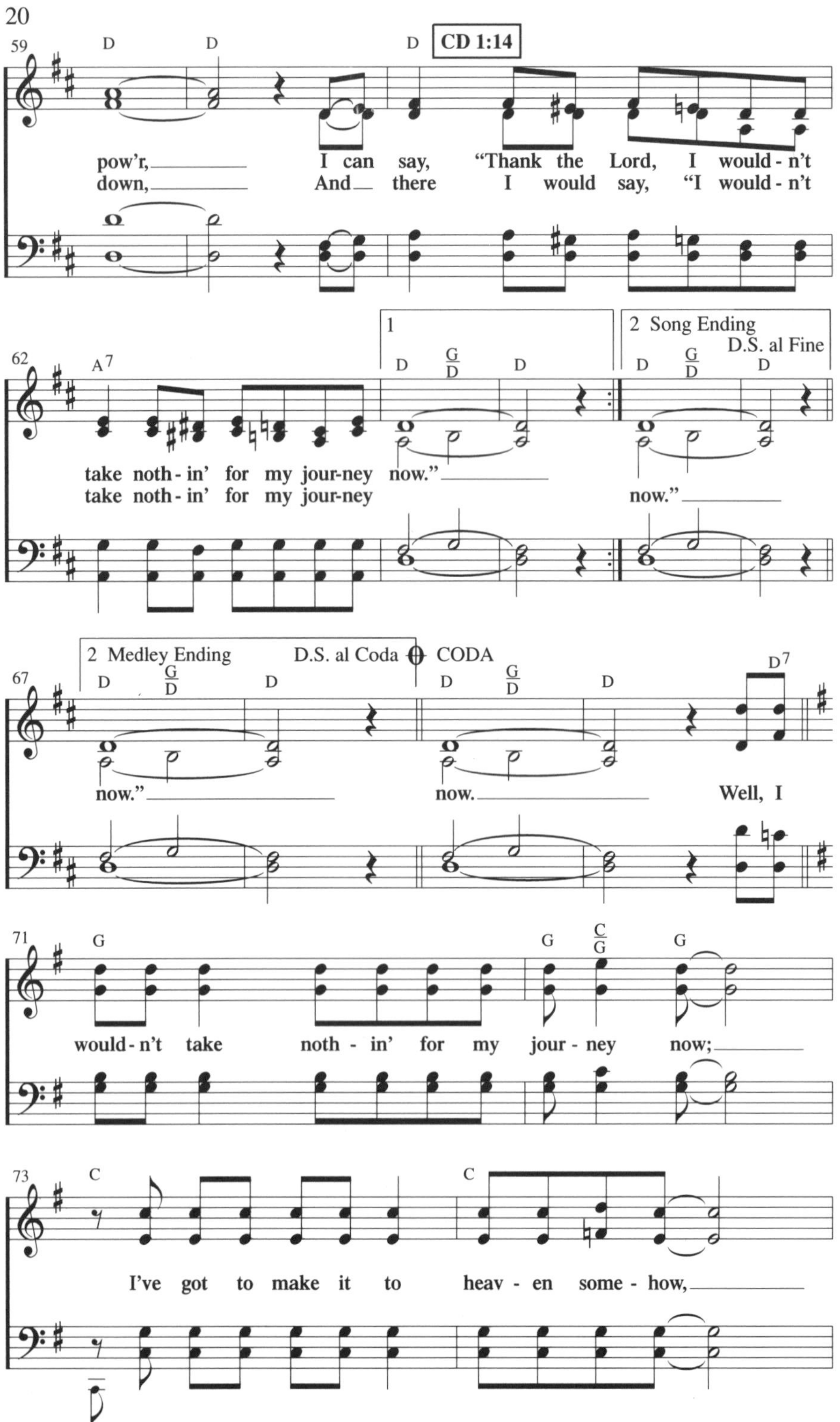
59
D D D CD 1:14
pow'r, I can say, "Thank the Lord, I would-n't
down, And there I would say, "I would-n't
62
A7
1
D G/D D
2 Song Ending
D.S. al Fine
D G/D D
take noth-in' for my jour-ney now."
take noth-in' for my jour-ney now."
2 Medley Ending
D.S. al Coda
CODA
67
D G/D D
D G/D D D7
now."
now.
Well, I
71
G G C/G G
would-n't take noth-in' for my jour-ney now;
73
C C
I've got to make it to heav-en some-how,

End of Medley

Daystar (Shine Down on Me)

S.R.

STEVE RICHARDSON
Arr. by Joseph Linn

Solo, with SATB backup throughout;
extended choral ending

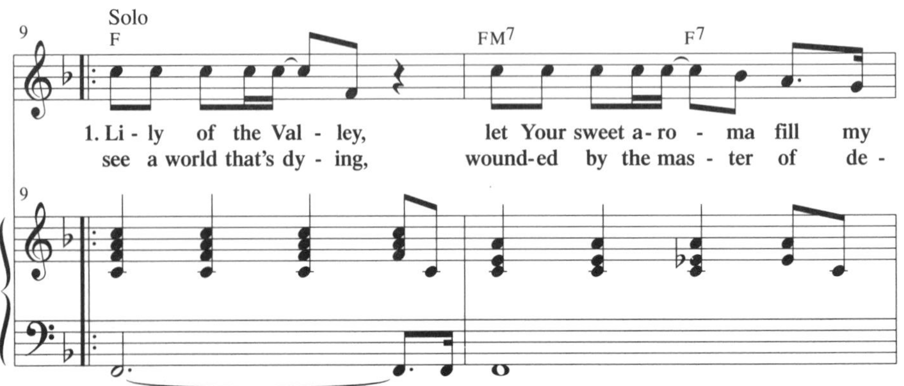

B♭
B♭
Gm
Gm9
Gm
life;
Rose of Shar-on, show me
ceit,
Grop-ing in the dark-ness,
Gm/F
C/E
B♭/D
how to grow in beau-ty in God's sight.
haunt-ed by the years of past de-feat.
C
Fsus/C
Fadd9
F
Fair-est of Ten Thou-sand,
But then I see You stand-ing near me, Lord,
Choir
Oo

18
F9
Bb
Bbm6
make me a reflec - tion of Your light; I pray
shin - ing with com - pas - sion in Your eyes; I pray
21
F
Gm
C7
Bb/C
C7sus C7
Day - star, shine down on me; let Your love shine thro' me in the
CD 1:16 1st time
CD 1:18 2nd time
23
F
F
Eb/F
F
CHORUS
Bb
night.
Lead me, Lord! I'll fol - low

B♭
C
C7/E
F
F
F♯
26
an - y- where You o - pen up the door.
G
G7
Em/G
G7
29
Let Your Word speak to me; show me what I've nev- er seen be -
C
C7
B♭/C
B♭add9/C
Fadd9
F
31
Lord, I want to be Your wit-ness!
31
fore.
31

35
FM7
F7
B♭
B♭m6
E♭ E
You can take what's wrong and make it right.
38
F
Gm
C
B♭/C
C7
Day-star, shine down on me; let Your love shine thro' me in the
CD 1:17
1
2 Song Ending
40
F
B♭add9/C
B♭/C
Fadd9
night.
2. Lord, I
night.

2 Extended Choral Ending
F
B♭
B♭m6
E♭
E
F
night.
Day - star, shine down on me;
2 Extended Choral Ending
night.
Day - star, shine down on me;
(solo continue on melody to the end)
Gm
C7
B♭/C
C7
F
let Your love shine thro' me in the night.
B♭m
B♭m6
E♭
E
F
mel.
Day - star, shine down on me;
Gm
rit.
C7
B♭/C
C7
F
F
let Your love shine thro' me in the night.

CHURCH TRIUMPHANT Medley

Arr. by Joseph Linn

I'M IN THIS CHURCH
SATB throughout; medley ending

TRIUMPHANTLY THE CHURCH WILL RISE
CHORUS: SATB
VERSE 2: 1st 2 phrases, men unison;
3rd phrase, ladies unison;
4th phrase, all unison
CHORUS: SATB
BRIDGE (3rd ending): SATB through "...His feet.";
unison through "...who's going?";
SATB on "Praise God, I am!"
CHORUS: SATB; coda

I'm in This Church

J.H. JOEL HEMPHILL

day, gon-na sail a - way; It's by His grace,
a - way, gon-na sail a - way.
Medley: 2nd time to Coda
Fine
not by my word, I'm in this church. When Je-sus
came, He was left out. There was no
Je - sus came, was left out.
place where He was wel - come here on earth. But He had a

39
G Am7 G/B Am7 G B/F♯ B7/F♯ Em Em/D Cm7 Cm
plan for a house that shall for - ev - er stand; He spoke these
had a plan
Song Ending: D.S. al Fine
Medley Ending: D.S. al Coda
43
G/D Em D/E A7 A7 D7 G C/G G C/D
words: "Up - on this rock I'll build my church." And I'm in this
church, my church."
CD 1:20
CODA
47
G Am7 G/B C D Cadd9/E D7/F♯ G G
church. I'm in this church.
I'm in this church.
Triumphantly the Church Will Rise
K.T.
CHORUS
KIRK TALLEY
51
Bm/D D7 G C/G G G/B D G D G
Tri - um - phant - ly the church will rise– Vic -

56
D/F♯ F°7 Cadd9/E E♭°7 G/D D7 G Bm/D D7 G Am7
to - rious meet - ing in the skies. See, the Fa - ther is
61
G/B D G B7/F♯ Em D/F♯ G Am7 G/B Dsus/C
read - y to wel - come His bride; Tri - um - phant - ly the
Medley: last time to Coda
66
G/D D7 G G Fine
1
G D7 D7
church will rise.
1. The stars dance with an - tic - i -
72
G G D7 Am7/E F♯°7 Em/G Am Em/B Em
pa - tion; The trem - bling clouds– they know it's time. Mu-

CD 1:21
78
E♭ Cm6 Cm Cm6/E♭ G/D G G/A A7sus
si - cians are tun - ing their in - stru - ments, And the sing - ers are
83
A7 D Gm/E E♯°7 D7/F♯
2
D7
hum - ming "Here Comes the Bride". 2. From ev - 'ry
88
D7 G G D7 Am7/E F♯°7 Em
na - tion they'll come, Tired from the race they have run,
94
Em Cm7 Cm6 Cm Cm/E♭ G/D D♯°7 Em
Bruised and bat - tered, wea - ry and worn, But
99
G/A A7sus A7 A7/C♯ D Gm/E E♯°7 D7/F♯
we shall be like Him on that res - ur - rec - tion morn.

End of Medley

ONE OF HIS OWN Medley

Arr. by Joseph Linn

I KNOW WHO HOLDS TOMORROW
VERSE 1: ladies unison through "...turn to gray.";
all unison through "...beside Him,";
remainder of verse, SATB (basses sing melody)
CHORUS: SATB
VERSE 3: solo
CHORUS: SATB; medley ending

ONE OF HIS OWN
VERSE 3: SAT
CHORUS: SATB; medley ending

I Know Who Holds Tomorrow

I.S. IRA STANPHILL

15
F F G/F F C C A+ A7
bor - row from its sun - shine, for its
bur - den's get - ting light - er; ev - 'ry
One who feeds the spar - row is the
19
D7 D7 D9 Bm/D D7 G7sus G7 F/G G7
skies may turn to gray. I don't
cloud is sil - ver - lined. There the
One who stands by me. And the
23
C C C° C F/C C C C9/E C7/E
wor - ry o'er the fu - ture, for I
sun is al - ways shin - ing; there no
path that be my por - tion may be
27
F F G/F F C C C9 C7
know what Je - sus said. And to -
tear will dim the eye At the
through the flame or flood; But His

31
F F G/F F C C F/A Fm6/A♭
day I'll walk be - side Him, for He
end - ing of the rain - bow, where the
pres - ence goes be - fore me, and I'm
CD 1:24 1st time
CD 1:26 2nd time
35
C/G Em/G G9 Em/G G7 C C
CHORUS
C9 C7
knows what is a - head.
moun - tains touch the sky. Man - y
cov - ered with His blood.
40
F F F° Dm/F F F/C C C C/B Am Am/G D9/F♯ D9 D7/E D7/F♯
things a - bout to - mor - row I don't seem to un - der -
seem, don't seem
46
Gsus G F/G G7 C C C9 C7 F F F/A Fm6/A♭
stand; But I know who holds to - mor - row, and I

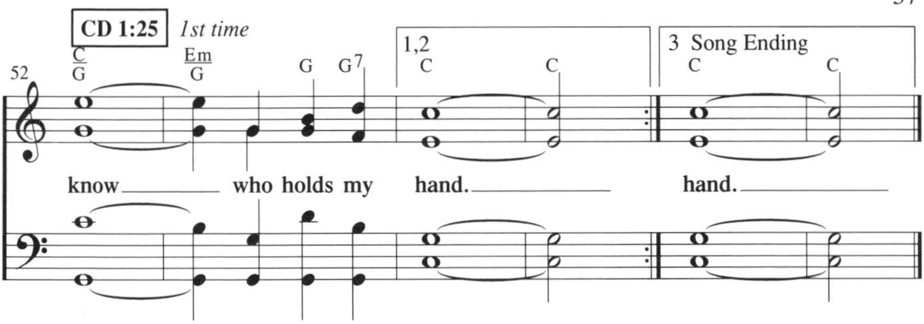

CD 1:25 *1st time*

1,2 — 3 Song Ending

52 C/G Em/G G G7 C C C C

know___ who holds my hand.___ hand.___

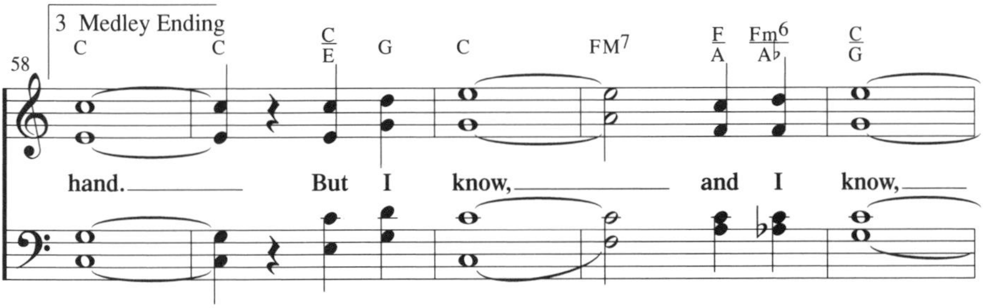

3 Medley Ending

58 C C C/E G C FM7 F/A Fm6/Ab C/G

hand.___ But I know,___ and I know,___

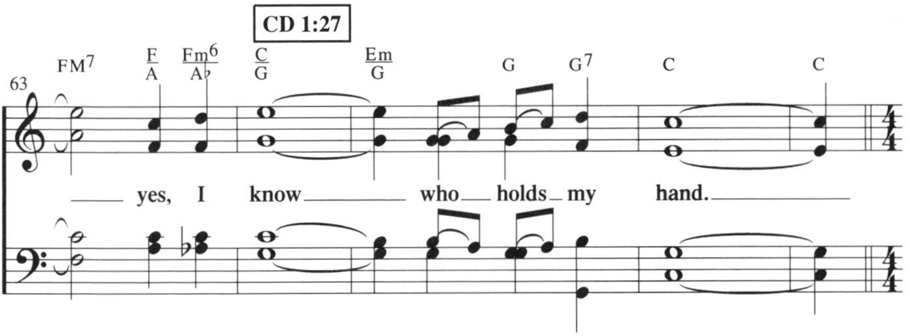

CD 1:27

63 FM7 F/A Fm6/Ab C/G Em/G G G7 C C

___ yes, I know___ who___ holds___ my hand.___

One of His Own

M.L. MOSIE LISTER

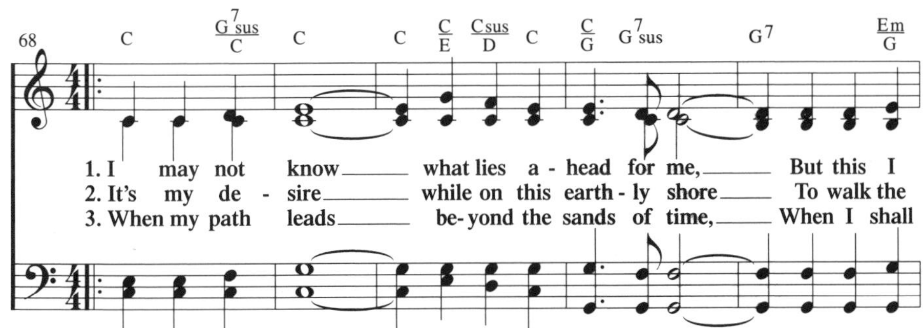

73
Dm Dm7 G9 Em/G G+ C C G7sus/C
know– I'm not a - lone. I've found a
road where He has gone. It's my de -
pass to worlds un - known, I'll climb the
77
C C C/E Csus/D C C/G G7sus G7 G F/G
Friend who al - ways stands by me, And claims me
sire to know that ev - er - more He'll keep me
stairs with His great hand in mine, Con - tent to
CD 1:28
81
G G G9 Em/G G7 C C
CHORUS
C G7/D C/E
as one of His own.
as one of His own. One of His
be one of His own.
86
F F F/A F F/C F/C C C Am7 A♭7
own is all I want to be; Where He may

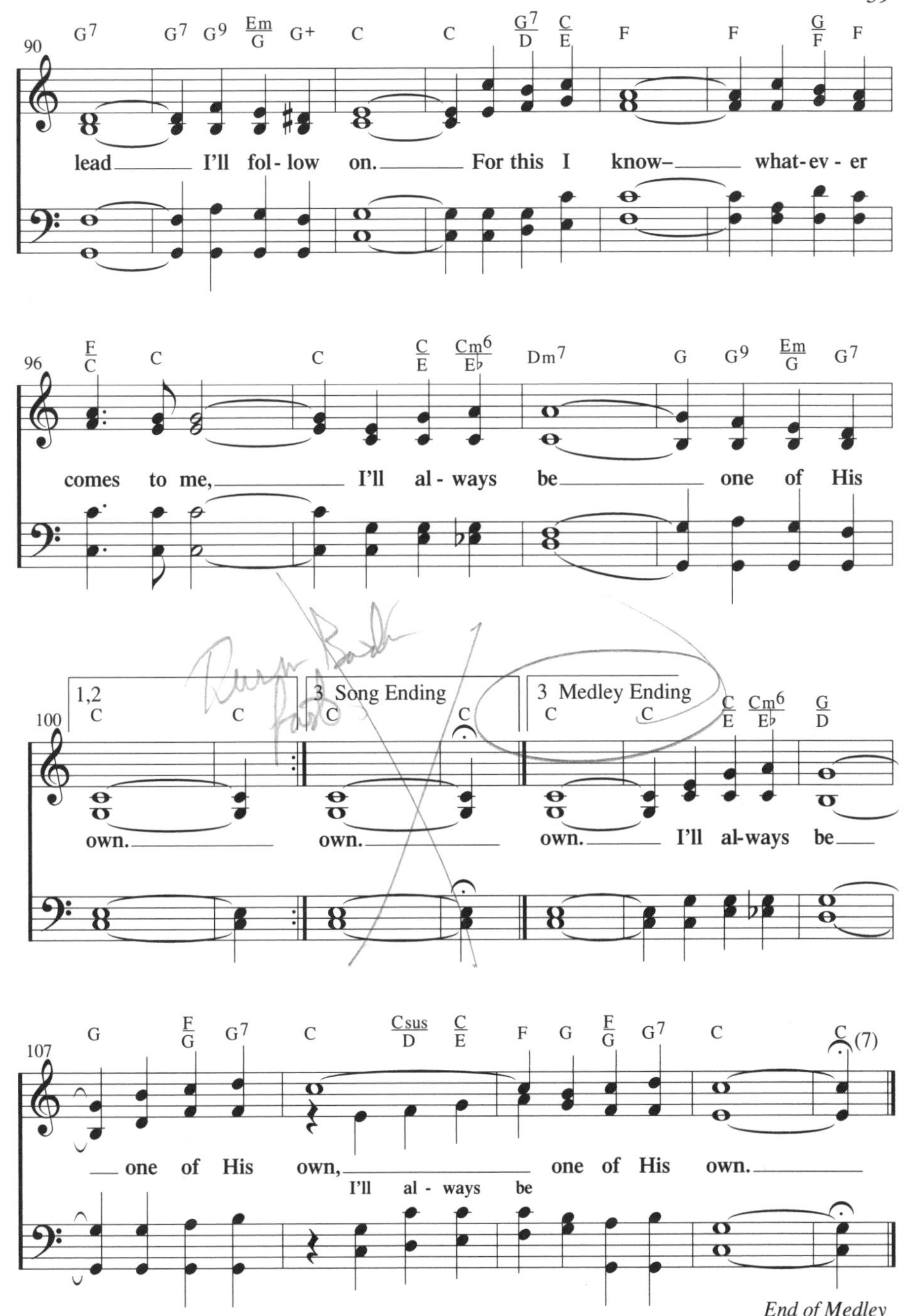
90
G7 G7 G9 Em/G G+ C C G7/D C/E F F G/F F
lead I'll fol-low on. For this I know– what-ev-er
96
F/C C C C/E Cm6/E♭ Dm7 G G9 Em/G G7
comes to me, I'll al-ways be one of His
100
1,2
C C
own.
3 Song Ending
C C
own.
3 Medley Ending
C C C/E Cm6/E♭ G/D
own. I'll al-ways be
107
G F/G G7 C Csus/D C/E F G F/G G7 C C (7)
one of His own, one of His own.
I'll al-ways be
End of Medley

The City Comin' Down

L.S.

VERSE 1: SATB
CHORUS: SATB
VERSE 2: SATB
CHORUS: SATB
VERSE 3: 1st phrase, solo 1; 2nd phrase, solo 2;
3rd phrase, SATB; 4th phrase, unison
CHORUS: unison; extended choral ending
CHORUS: SATB; coda

LAVANUL SHERRILL
Arr. by Joseph Linn

14
A♭ A♭/C B♭ E♭ Cm/E♭
in the sky they will al - most baf-fle your mind. But the
moun - tain, gon-na cross on the des - ert sand. Well,
has - see– you can name them by the score. I don't
17
A♭ A♭°7 A♭ A♭ C C7
time's gon-na turn, and they're all gon-na burn and no-where will be
Lot went down to Sod - om, but not old A-bra-
have a big in - vest - ment, no man-sion way up-
20
Fm A♭/E♭ A♭7/E♭ D♭ A♭ Fm
found. I'm gon-na be up in that cit - y that
ham– He was look-in' for that cit - y that
town; But I've got one in that cit - y that
23
B♭9 D♭/E♭ A♭ E♭+ A♭ A♭°7
CHORUS
John saw com-in' down. I'm not look-in' for a cit-y that's a-

27
A♭
D♭7
A♭
E♭+
go - in' up, but the one that's com - in' down. I'm not
30
A♭
A♭°7
A♭
A♭/C
put - tin' my trust in the one that will crum - ble and
32
B♭7
E♭
E♭+
A♭
A♭°7
A♭
A♭°7
fall down to the ground. But I'm head - in' for the one that the
35
A♭
B♭m/A♭
A♭
A♭
C7/G
Fm
A♭/E♭
Lord has made and is built e - ter - nal - ly sound. I'm not
CD 1:30
1st time
CD 1:31
2nd time
Extended choral ending: last time to Coda
38
D♭
A♭
A♭
Fm
Fm7
look - in' for a cit - y go - in' up, but the

1,2
3 Song Ending
3 Extended Choral Ending
D.S. al Coda
CODA
B♭9
D♭
E♭
A♭
A♭7
A♭7
C
D♭
Fm
Fm7
E♭9sus
E♭7
N.C.
one that's com - in' down.
I'm not
look - in' for a cit - y go - in' up, but the one that's com - in'
down.
down, the one that's com - in' down.

ALL THE GLORY Medley

Arr. by Joseph Linn

ALL THE GLORY BELONGS TO JESUS
VERSE 1: ladies unison
CHORUS: SATB
VERSE 2: ladies unison
CHORUS: SATB; medley ending

HE'S THE LORD OF GLORY
CHORUS: SATB
VERSE 3: unison
CHORUS: SATB; coda

All the Glory Belongs to Jesus

12
fear.
But from our man - y
throne.
Our Lord will be the
D♭add9
G♭m add9 / D♭
D♭add9
15
dif-f'renc-es, His love has made us one. This
sun and moon of shin - ing end-less days. The
G♭m add9 / D♭
D♭
D♭/C G♭/B♭
D♭add9 / A♭
CD 1:33 1st time
CD 1:35 2nd time
18
song we share has on - ly just be - gun.
heav-ens then will ech-o when we sing.
D♭/E♭
E♭7sus
E♭7
Cm/E♭
E♭7
A♭sus
A♭7

CHORUS
N.C.
22
All the glo - ry be-longs to Je - sus.
26
All the praise be-longs to Him.
30
All that I am all that I am, all that I am or ev-er hope to be,
1 CD 1:34
34
All the glo - ry be-longs to Him.
2 Song Ending
39
glo - ry be - longs to Him.

He's the Lord of Glory

P.C.S.

PHYLLIS C. SPIERS

59
D A7 G/B A/C♯ A7/C♯ A7 D Em7 E♯°7
AM. He's the Al- pha and O - me- ga, the Be - gin- ning and the
63
D/F♯ G G D G/D D Em/D D F♯m7/C♯
End. His name is Won- der- ful; the Prince of Peace is He, the
Medley: last time to Coda
68
Bm Gm/B♭ Gm6/B♭ D/A A9 F♯m/A A7 D D
Fine
Ev - er - last - ing Fa- ther through- out e - ter - ni - ty.
73
D D D
1. Be - hold, what man - ner of Man is this who
2. Be - hold, what man - ner of Man is this who
3. Be - hold, what man - ner of Man is this who
4. Be - hold, what man - ner of Man is this who

76
G6
G
G6
D
stands be - tween God and man? His
sits up - on His heav - en - ly throne? He
spoke to the wom - an at the well: "Ev - er -
speaks to the maimed and halt? He
78
D
A7sus
D
D
eyes are as a flame of fire; His
rules and reigns from heav'n a - bove His be -
last - ing life I'll give to thee, far
says, "Thy sins be for - giv - en thee; take
80
Bm6
E7
B
E7
E9
A
F#m
A
D
fan is in His hand. John saw Him in the sev - en
lov - ed and His own. He's the Li - on of the tribe of
rich-er than man can tell. And who - so - e'er shall
up thy bed and walk." He stands as the might - y
83
D
G6
G
G6
D
church-es as the sun in bril - lian - cy.
Ju - dah; the Root of Dav - id is He.
drink of the well shall live e - ter - nal - ly."
Heal - er, and He cries, "Look un - to Me."

End of Medley

WHO AM I? Medley

Arr. by Joseph Linn

TOO PRECIOUS
VERSE 1: solo
CHORUS: SATB
VERSE 2: solo
CHORUS: SATB; medley ending

WHO AM I?
CHORUS: SATB
VERSE 1: SATB through "...such disgrace,";
remainder of verse, SATB (basses sing melody)
CHORUS: SATB; coda

Too Precious

D.W. DAN WHITTEMORE

14
G G F/A G7/B C C G/D
I owned the rich-est of king-doms,___ Still I could not save___ my-
on-ly the love of my Sav-ior___ That re-deems me from my
19
D7 C/D D7 C/G G Am7 G/B C D D9
CHORUS
self from my sin.___
sin and its grave.___
Too pre-cious by far to be
25
G G G/F♯ Em Em7 A9 A A9 Am Bm7 Am/C D7
sold,___ Or_ ran-somed for mere earth-ly gold–___ If
CD 1:38
1st time
31
G Bm/D D7 G G/B C G/B Am Am/C G/D
wealth were the way, all earth could not pay___ The price that could

36
D9
Bm/D
D7
1
C/G
G
Am/G
G
2 Song Ending
C/G
G
Am/G
G
save a man's soul.
soul.
41
2 Medley Ending
C/G
G
Am/G
G
G
Em
soul.
41
2 Medley Ending
Even eighths
CD 1:39
45
Em
Am
Em/A
F♯m/A
A9
D
D/A
G/A
D

Who Am I?

C.G.
CHORUS
CHARLES (RUSTY) GOODMAN
Who am I that a King would bleed and die for? Who am
I that He would pray, "Not my will, Thine." for? The an-swer
I may nev-er know– why He ev-er loved me so, That to an
CD 1:40
1st time
Medley: last time to Coda
Fine
old rug-ged cross He'd go, for who am I?
N.C.
1. When I think of how He came so far from glo-ry,
2. Then I'm re-mind-ed of His words, "I'll leave thee nev-er.

D
Bm/D
F♯7/C♯
Bm
Bm7
C♯m/E
E7
71
Came and dwelt a - mong the low - ly such as
Just be true; I'll give to you a life for -
A
Bm7
A/C♯
N.C.
D
A7
D
74
I, To suf - fer shame and such dis - grace, On Mount
ev - er." I won - der what I could have done To de -
G
G/B
A
G/A
D
D
D°
D
A7
G/A
A7
78
Cal - v'ry take my place, Then I ask my - self a ques - tion, "Who am
serve God's on - ly Son– Fight my bat - tles 'til they're won– who am
1
2 Song Ending D.S. al Fine
2 Medley Ending D.S. al Coda
82
I?"
I?
I?
CODA
88
I?
Who am
I?
End of Medley

Holy Highway

J.H. and G.H.

JIM and GINGER HENDRICKS
Arr. by Joseph Linn

VERSE 1: SATB
CHORUS: unison
VERSE 2: SATB
CHORUS: unison; 2nd ending
BRIDGE: SATB
VERSE 1: SATB (basses sing melody); coda, SATB

CD 1:41

14
E♭ E♭ A♭
last - ing joy up - on them, there's a rem - nant strong and
ban - ners in the vic - t'ry; raise them high– His word is
17
E♭ E♭9 A♭ E♭ Cm7
true. We bring the song back to Zi - on; we bring the
true. We bring our song back to Zi - on; we bring the
3rd time to Coda
CHORUS
20
Fm Gm/B♭ B♭7 E♭ E♭ E♭ E♭ A♭/E♭
praise back to You.
praise back to You.
We ex - alt You, God Al - might - y; You are
26
B♭7/E♭ E♭ E♭ A♭/E♭
wor - thy to be praised. Let all na - tions bow be - fore You, Ho - ly
CD 1:42
CD 1:43
30
B♭7/E♭ E♭M7 B♭7/E♭
1 E♭ E♭
2 E♭ E♭ Cm Cm/B♭
a bit more legato
An - cient of all days.
days.
Ho - ly, ho - ly,

36
A♭
B♭/D
B♭
B♭7
A♭/E♭
E♭
Cm
Cm/B♭
ho - ly, Lord God Al - might - y, Ho - ly, ho - ly,
40
A♭
B♭7sus
B♭7
p-mp-mf-f
CD 1:44
4th time
N.C.
N.C.
Hal - le - lu - jah.
ho - ly is the Lord.
Hal - le - lu - jah, hal - le -
Hal - le - lu - jah,
Hal - le - lu - jah, hal - le -
1-3
4
D.S. al Coda
45
A♭M9
A♭
B♭/A♭
E♭/G
E♭/G
E♭/G
lu - jah, hal - le - lu - jah. jah.
hal - le - lu - jah. jah.
lu - jah.
CODA
50
E♭
E♭9
A♭
E♭
Cm
Fm
Gm/B♭
B♭7
You. We bring the song back to Zi - on; we bring the praise back to
54
E♭
A♭6
A♭6/G
Fm7
B♭7sus
B♭7
E♭
E♭
E♭
E♭
(7)
You. We bring the praise back to You.

BOUND FOR THE KINGDOM Medley

Arr. by Joseph Linn

PEACE IN THE VALLEY
VERSE 1: SATB (basses sing melody)
CHORUS: SATB; medley ending

I'M BOUND FOR THE KINGDOM
VERSE 1: 1st half, unison; 2nd half, SAT
CHORUS: SATB
VERSE 2: 1st half, unison; 2nd half, SAT
CHORUS: SATB; medley ending

Peace in the Valley

T.A.D. THOMAS A. DORSEY

14
A♭ G♭/A♭ D♭ D♭ G♭
yes. Well, the morn - ing is bright and the Lamb is the
yes. Well, the sun ev - er beams in the val - ley of
yes. Well, the beast from the wild shall be led by a
CD 1: 46
18
D♭ D♭ E♭7/B♭ A♭7
Light, And the night, night is as fair as the
dreams, And no clouds there will ev - er be
child, And I'll be changed, changed from this crea - ture that I
CHORUS
21
D♭ G♭ D♭ N.C. G♭ G♭
day, oh, yes.
seen, oh, yes. There will be peace in the val - ley for
am, oh, yes.
26
D♭ G♭/D♭ D♭ A♭7 D♭ E♭9/B♭ E♭9
me some - day. There will be peace in the val - ley for

30 A♭ B♭m6 A♭ G♭/A♭ D♭

me, O Lord, I pray. There'll be no sad - ness, no

no

33 D♭/F D♭ G♭ E♭7

sor - row, no trou - ble I'll see. There will be

sor - row, O my Lord - y, no trou - ble, trou - ble I'll see.

36 D♭ B♭7 B♭m6 A♭7 | 1,2 D♭ G♭/D♭ D♭ | 3 Song Ending D♭ G♭/D♭ D♭

peace in the val - ley for me. me,

me, for me. me, for me.

3 Medley Ending

42 D♭ B♭m7 B♭m6 A♭7 G♭7 D♭ D♭ B♭/D E♭m Em

Peace in the

me, in the val - ley for me.

Peace in the

42 3 Medley Ending

I'm Bound for the Kingdom

M.L. — MOSIE LISTER

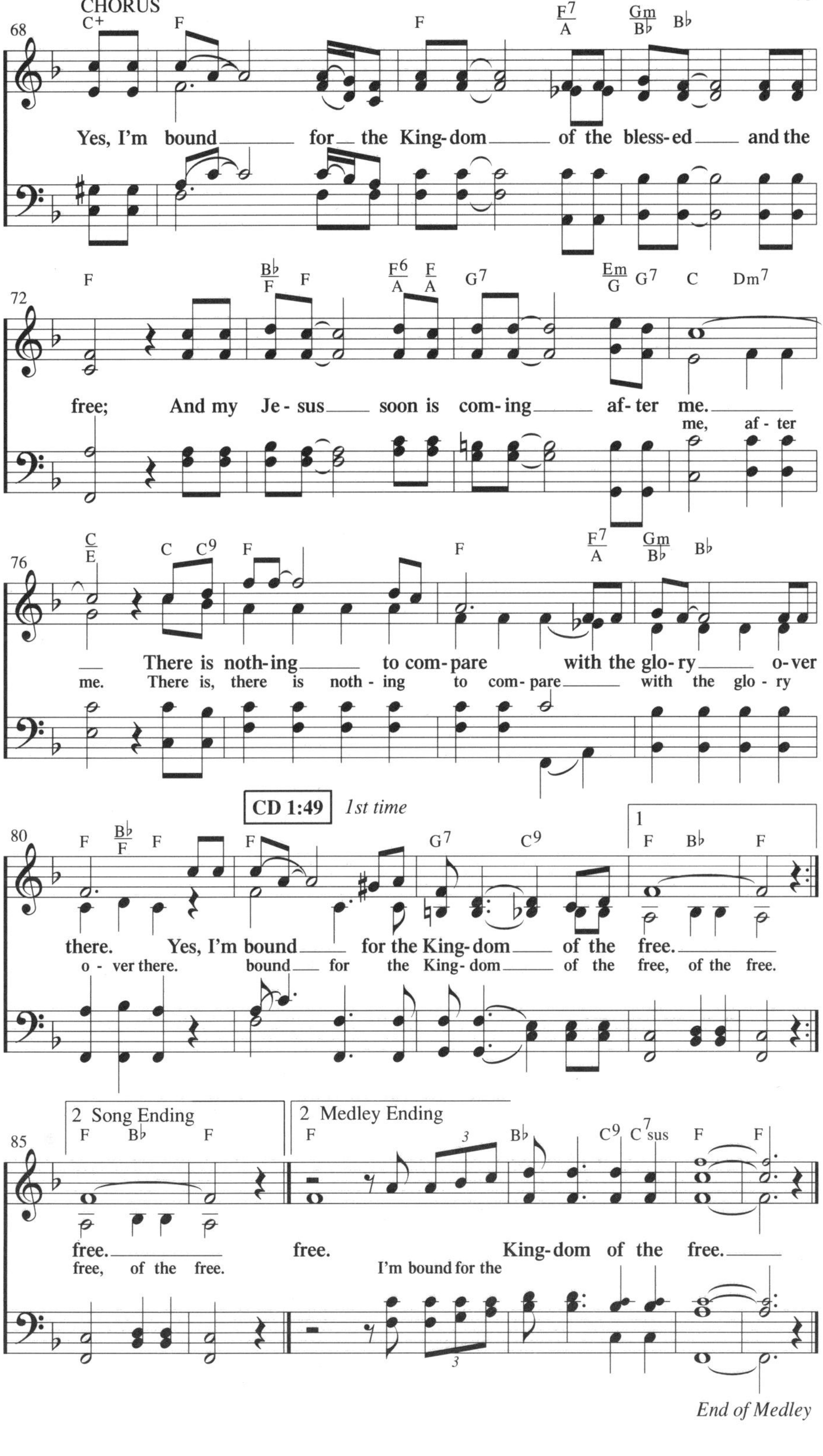
CHORUS
68
C+ F F F7/A Gm/B♭ B♭
Yes, I'm bound for the King-dom of the bless-ed and the
72
F B♭/F F F6/A F/A G7 Em/G G7 C Dm7
free; And my Je-sus soon is com-ing af-ter me.
me, af-ter
76
C/E C C9 F F F7/A Gm/B♭ B♭
There is noth-ing to com-pare with the glo-ry o-ver
me. There is, there is noth-ing to com-pare with the glo-ry
CD 1:49
1st time
80
F B♭/F F F G7 C9
1
F B♭ F
there. Yes, I'm bound for the King-dom of the free.
o-ver there. bound for the King-dom of the free, of the free.
85
2 Song Ending
F B♭ F
2 Medley Ending
F B♭ C9 C7sus F F
free. free. King-dom of the free.
free, of the free. I'm bound for the
End of Medley

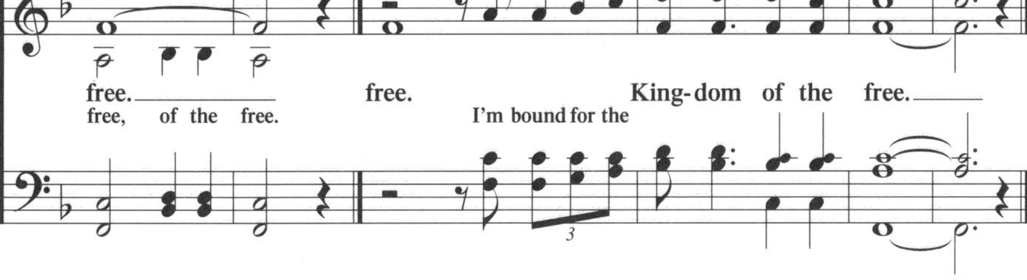

SWEET DELIVERANCE Medley

Arr. by Joseph Linn

AT THE CROSSING
VERSE 1: SAT
CHORUS: SATB; medley ending

IN THE ARMS OF SWEET DELIVERANCE
CHORUS: SATB
VERSE 1: unison
CHORUS: SATB
VERSE 2: unison; medley ending
CHORUS: SATB; coda

At the Crossing

M.L. MOSIE LISTER

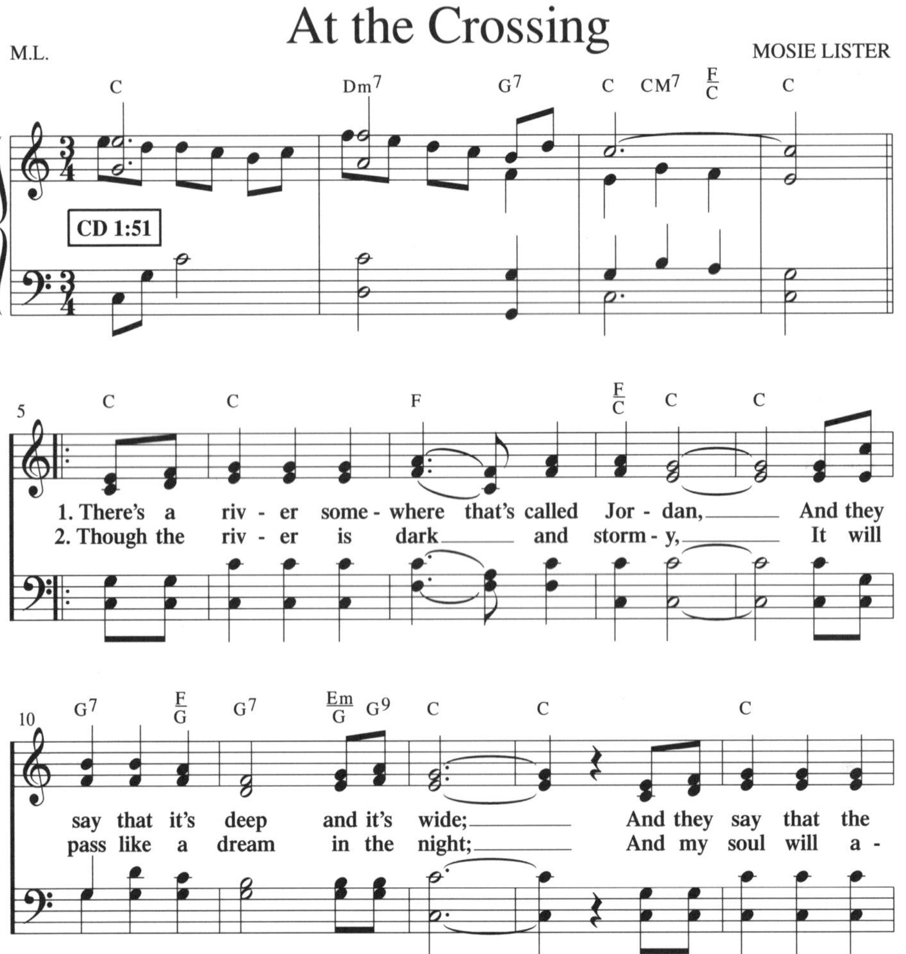

15
king and the beg-gar On that shore will stand side by
wake in the morn-ing In re-gions of end-less de-
20
CHORUS
side.
light.
At the cross-ing of the Jor-dan, Why should
27
I be a-fraid? There'll be Some-one there who loves me to
31
guide me 'cross the riv-er to end-less joys a-
1
2 Song Ending
2 Medley Ending
37
bove. bove. bove.
bove, a-bove. bove, a-bove. bove, a-bove.
He will

CD 1:52

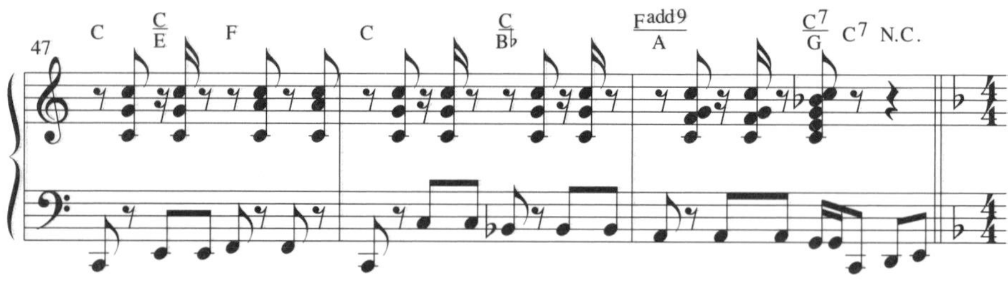

In the Arms of Sweet Deliverance

M.L.

MOSIE LISTER

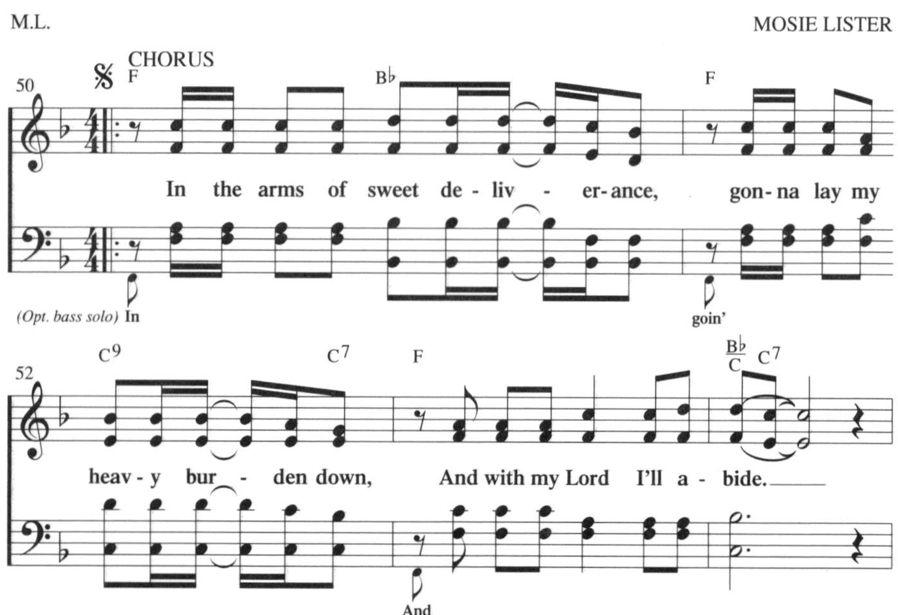

55
F
B♭
F
When at last my trav - lin' days are done, In the land some -
When
In
57
C9
F
C9
where be - yond the sun, In the arms of sweet de - liv - er - ance,
In
Medley: last time to Coda
59
F
C9
F
B♭/F
F/C
C7
F
Fine
In the arms of sweet de - liv - er - ance, I shall rest by and by.
In
I
62
N.C.
F
C7
1. Of trou - bles I've had much more than e - nough;
2. I've read in the Book how the Lord once said, "The
64
F
B♭
Man - y the days my path is rough;
rain will fall on the good and the bad, But

65
F/C
Dm7/C
C7
F
N.C.
Man - y the days I won - der what to do. But
wise is the man who waits up - on the Lord." When
67
F
C7
then I talk to my God in prayer, And
trials and sor - rows mul - ti - ply, I
68
F
B♭
He as - sures me that He's right there, And
will not ask Him the rea - son why, For
CD 1:53
1st time
CD 1:54
2nd time
1
2 Song Ending
D.S. al Fine
2 Medley Ending
D.S. al Coda
69
F/C
C7
F
what - so - ev - er may come He'll see me thro'.
strength is mine on - ly heav - en can af - ford. ford.
CODA
73
F
B♭/F
F/C
C7
rit.
(8)
by. I shall rest by and by. I shall rest by and by.
I
I
End of Medley

RESCUED Medley

Arr. by Joseph Linn

THE LIGHTHOUSE
VERSE 1: solo
CHORUS: SATB; medley ending

IT'S DIFFERENT NOW
VERSE 1: unison through "...I'm free.";
remainder of verse, SATB
CHORUS: SATB; medley ending
CHORUS: SATB; ending 5 (continuation of medley ending)

TOUCHED BY THE HAND OF THE LORD
VERSE 1: SATB
CHORUS: SATB
VERSE 2: 1st half, SA;
2nd half, men unison
CHORUS: SATB; medley ending

The Lighthouse

RONNIE HINSON

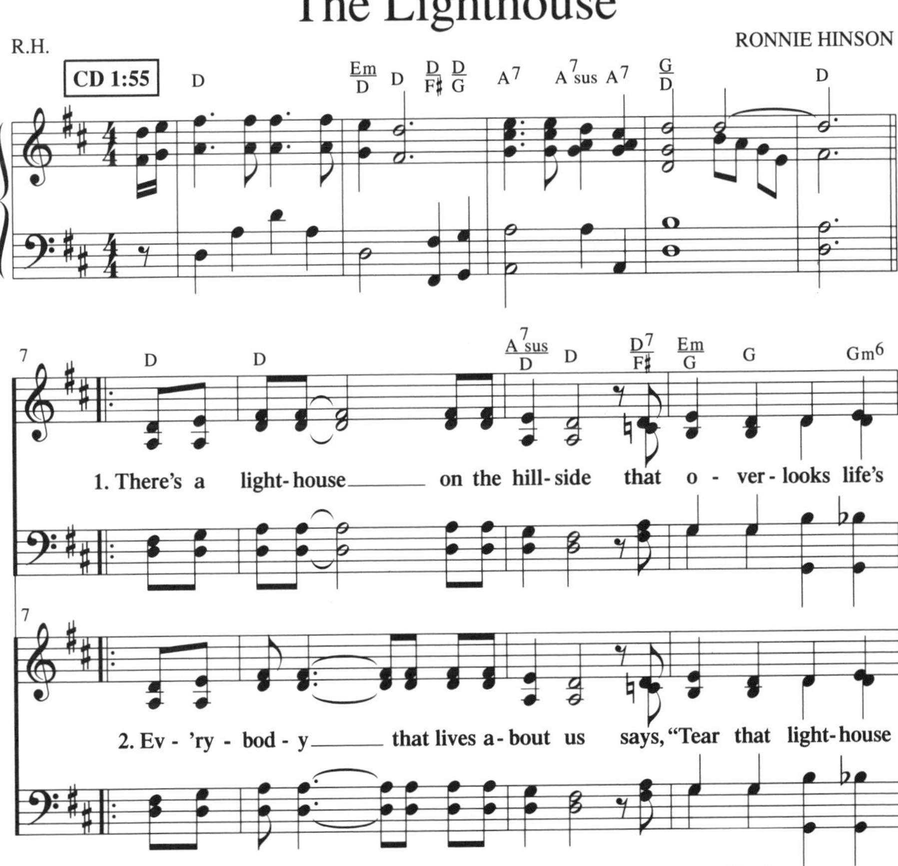

11
D
D
A7sus
D
D
sea. When I'm tossed, it sends out a light
11
down. The big ships don't sail this way an-y-more; there's no

14
E7
E6
E7
A
F♯m
A
A7
D
Bm
D
that I might see. And the light that shines in
14
use of it stand-ing round." Then my mind goes back to that

17
D7 D9 G G/A A7
dark - ness now will safe - ly lead us o'er. If it
17
storm - y night, when just in time I saw the light– Yes, the
CD 1:56
20
D A7sus/D D D7/F♯ Em/G G/A A7 D
was - n't for the light - house, my ship would be no more.
20
light from that old light - house that stands up there on the hill.
CHORUS
24
D A7/D D F♯m/A A9 Em/D D D9 G Gm6
And I thank God for the light - house; I owe my life to

28
D D F♯m/A A9 Em/D D Bm6 E/B E E9 A F♯m/A A7
Him. For Je - sus is the light-house, and from the rocks of sin He has
33
D F♯m/A A9 Em/D D D9 G A9♭ D G/A A7 D
shone a light a - round me that I could clear-ly see– If it was-n't for the
38
A7/D D N.C.
light-house,
tell me,
1
Em/A G/A A7 D
where would this ship be?
2 Song Ending
Em/A G/A A7 D
where would this ship be?
43
2 Medley Ending
Em/A G/A D D D G/D D
where would this ship be?

It's Different Now

D.B. DAVID BEATTY

CD 1:57

1. Once I was lost in sin; I had no peace with - in. To
save my wea - ry soul, I knew not how. But Je - sus came to me, and
by His grace I'm free.

2. I went to church one day, to hear them sing and pray; The
preach - er firm - ly plowed the gos - pel plow. He said, "You must re - pent," so
down the aisle I went.

3. Sin's fet - ters held me fast; the die was al - most cast. My
proud and haugh - ty spir - it would not bow. But just one glimpse of Him– it
broke the pow'r of sin.

4. And now my hopes are bright; I praise Him day and night. How
He could change me so I knew not how. But praise the Lord, it's done– the
vic - t'ry now is won!

Now it's dif - f'rent; yes, it's oh, ___ so dif - f'rent

CHORUS
N.C.
E♭
A♭/E♭
B♭7
It's dif-f'rent now since Je - sus saved my
now.
Yes, it's dif-f'rent now,
soul; It's dif-f'rent now since by His blood I'm
since He saved my soul.
Yes, it's dif-f'rent now;
whole. Old Sa - tan had to flee when
Fm7
E♭/G
by His blood I'm whole.
Ah,
Ah,
CD 1:58
1st time
A♭
E♭/B♭
A♭/B♭
Je - sus res - cued me.
Ah,
Now it's dif - f'rent; yes it's

1-3
4 Song Ending
4 Medley Ending
D.S.
oh, so dif- f'rent now.
now.
now.
5 (continuation of medley ending)
N.C.
It's oh, so dif - f'rent. Yes, it's oh, so dif- f'rent
now!
CD 1:59

Touched by the Hand of the Lord

M.L. MOSIE LISTER

End of Medley

GOLDEN STAIRS Medley

Arr. by Joseph Linn

OH, WHAT A HAPPY DAY
VERSE 1: SAT
CHORUS: SATB
VERSE 2: SAT
CHORUS: SATB; medley ending

I'LL WALK DEM GOLDEN STAIRS
CHORUS: SATB
VERSE 2: solo, with SATB background vocals
CHORUS: SATB
VERSE 3: solo, with SATB background vocals
CHORUS: SATB; coda

16
D
Em/D
D
D9
G
Em/G
G
D
take my Sav-ior's hand in that bless-ed prom-ised land, I'll
streets of pur-est gold; I'll live for-ev-er and not grow old. I'll
20
Em/D
C♯/D
D
Em/D
Bm6
A7
D
G/D
D
shout and sing thro' the end-less a-ges, "Oh, what a hap-py day!"
shout and sing thro' the end-less a-ges, "Oh, what a hap-py day!"
CHORUS
25
D
Em/D
C♯/D
D
D
D9
G
Em/G
G
G/B
Oh, what a hap-py day that will be when we gath-er
What a hap-py day
29
D
N.C.
D
D
D
G/D
D
there. Oh, what a hap-py day when we climb those gold-en
What a hap-py day
33
A
A
D/A
Em/A
C♯/A
D
Em/D
D
D9
stairs. We'll meet with those who have gone be-fore, James and

CD 2:2
1st time
37
G
Em
G
G
D
Em
D
D
Bm6
A7
John and a mil- lion more. What a hap- py time that's sure to be; oh, what a hap- py
41
1
G
D
D
2 Song Ending
G
D
D
day.
What a hap- py day.
day.
What a hap- py day.
47
2 Medley Ending
G
D
G
D
D
G
day.
What a hap- py day.
What a hap- py day! What a hap- py
50
D
D
D
D
day!

I'll Walk Dem Golden Stairs

C.H. CULLY HOLT

78
E♭7 B♭ B♭ B♭
me, "Well done," And all my cares are laid
lone-some, wear-y road. Some-times I can't help but
I can hard-ly wait To reach that sweet bye and
Oo,
dmm, dmm, dmm, dmm, Dmm, dmm, dmm, dmm, dmm,

82
F6 F7 F7 B♭ B♭
by, I'll lay down my sword; my
cry. I'll ne'er re-gret a
bye. But now I see those
Oo
dmm, dmm, dmm, dmm, dmm, dmm, dmm, Dmm, dmm, dmm, dmm, dmm,

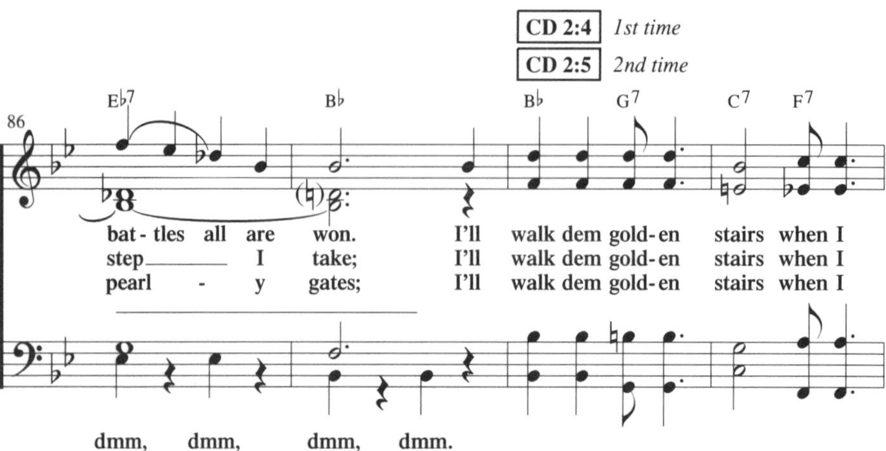
CD 2:4 1st time
CD 2:5 2nd time
86
E♭7 B♭ B♭ G7 C7 F7
bat-tles all are won. I'll walk dem gold-en stairs when I
step I take; I'll walk dem gold-en stairs when I
pearl-y gates; I'll walk dem gold-en stairs when I
dmm, dmm, dmm, dmm.

90
B♭
B♭m6
1,2
die. Well, well, well,
B♭
3 Song Ending: D.S. al Fine
Medley Ending: D.S. al Coda
die. Well, well, well,
B♭
die, when I die.
die, when I die.
die, when I die.
CODA
93
B♭
C7
B♭/F
G7
C7
B♭/F
G7
die. I'm gon-na walk dem gold-en stairs, climb dem gold-en
97
C7
C7/G
B♭/F
G7
Gm/C
F9sus
F7
stairs, I'm gon-na walk dem gold-en stairs when I
100
B♭
B♭
B♭
B♭
die.
100
End of Medley

GOD UNDERSTANDS MY TEARS Medley

Arr. by Joseph Linn

TEARS ARE A LANGUAGE
VERSE 1: ladies unison
CHORUS: SATB
VERSE 2: men unison
CHORUS: SATB; medley ending

HE WASHED MY EYES WITH TEARS
VERSE 2: SAT through "...the sands.";
remainder of verse, SATB;
medley ending

Tears Are a Language

G.J. GORDON JENSEN

18
C
C6
Em/B
Cm6/A
G/D
Am7
CM7/D
D7
G
G
Tears are a lan - guage God un - der - stands.
Tears are a lan - guage God un - der - stands.
CHORUS
23
G
Gsus/A
G/B
C
Am/C
C
G
Gsus/A
God sees the tears of a bro - ken - heart - ed soul.
27
G/B
G/D
G
D/F♯
Em
Bm7
D/C
C
G/C
C
G
D7/A
D7
Bm/D
D7
Gsus/D
He sees your tears and hears them when they fall. God weeps a -
32
G
D7sus/G
G
G
Am7
G/B
Am/C
CM7
Am/C
Am/C
Em/B
Cm6/A
long with man, and takes him by the hand. Tears are a

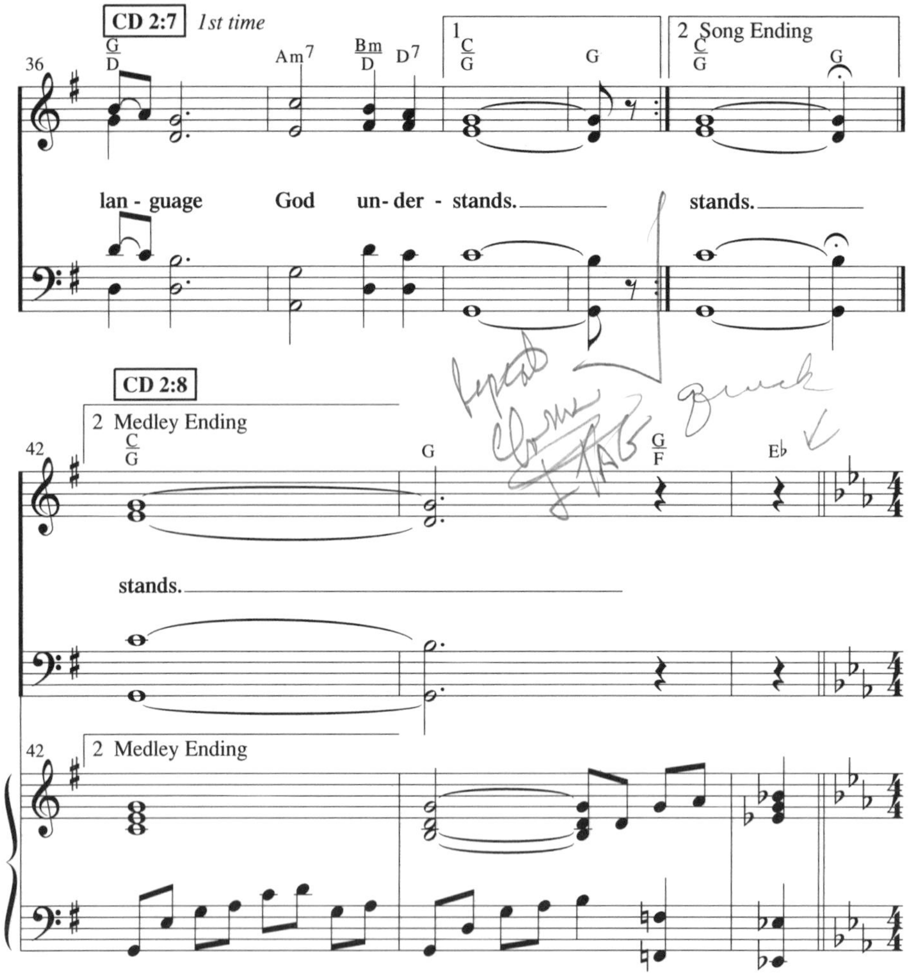
CD 2:7
1st time
1
2 Song Ending
G/D Am7 Bm/D D7 C/G G C/G G
36
lan - guage God un- der - stands. stands.
CD 2:8
2 Medley Ending
C/G G G/F E♭
42
stands.
42
2 Medley Ending

He Washed My Eyes with Tears

I.S. IRA STANPHILL

E♭ E♭° E♭ Cm/E♭ E♭ E♭ Fm7/B♭
45
1. He washed my eyes with tears that I might see
2. He washed my eyes with tears that I might see

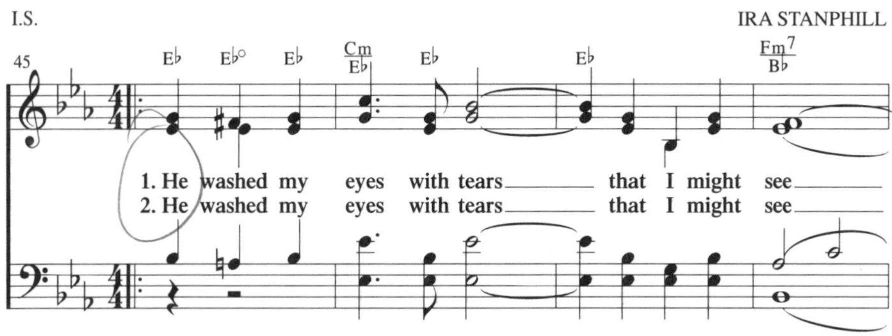

49
B♭ B♭7 B♭°7 B♭7 Gm/B♭ G♭/B♭ Fm/B♭ Fm/B♭ B♭7 A♭/B♭ B♭7 E♭
The bro-ken heart I had was good for me.
The glo-ry of Him-self re-vealed to me.
53
E♭ E♭° E♭ Cm/E♭ E♭ E♭ B♭7sus
He tore it all a-part and looked in-side;
I did not know that He had wound-ed hands;
57
B♭7 B♭°7 B♭7 Gm/B♭ G♭/B♭ Fm/B♭ Fm/B♭ B♭7 A♭/B♭ B♭7 E♭ E♭
He found it full of fear and fool-ish pride.
I saw the blood He spilt up-on the sands.
62
E♭ B♭7/F E♭7/G A♭ A♭ A♭M9 A♭ E♭ E♭ Cm Cm7♯ Cm7
He swept a-way the things that made me blind; And then I
I saw the marks of shame and wept and cried. He was my

End of Medley

FREE INDEED Medley

Arr. by Joseph Linn

FREE INDEED
VERSE 1: unison
CHORUS: SATB
VERSE 2: unison
CHORUS: SATB; medley ending

HE SET ME FREE
VERSE 1: SATB
CHORUS: SATB
VERSE 2: SATB
CHORUS: SATB; medley ending

Free Indeed

D.M. DALE MATHEWS

14
G C/G G Am/G G C/G G G7 Am/C C
Spir - it - filled re - viv - al go - ing on to - day, with a mes - sage for you and
Spir - it of the Lord moved in - to my life, there's been a ___ change in
17
C#°7 G/D G G/F# Em Em7 Em A9 D7 C/D G
me: He whom the Son sets free ___ is free in - deed.
me. He whom the Son sets free ___ is free in - deed.
CHORUS
22
G D/G G D7 G B7 C G
He whom the Son sets free ___ is free in - deed. ___
26
Bm Em D/E Em Em7 A9 D7
He whom the Son sets free ___ is free in - deed. ___
30
G Am/G G7 G7 G° G7 B7 C C#°7
You shall know the truth, ___ and the truth shall make you free!

CD 2:10
1st time
34
G/D G Bm7/F♯ Em Em7 Em A9 D7
1 G
2 Song Ending G
He whom the Son sets free is free in - deed. deed.
39
2 Medley Ending
G G Em/G G G
deed. He whom the Son sets free, He whom the
43
G G/D G Bm7/F♯ Em Em7 Em A9 CM7/D D7
Son sets free, He whom the Son sets free is free, free in -

CD 2: 11
48
G
G
E♭7
deed.
48

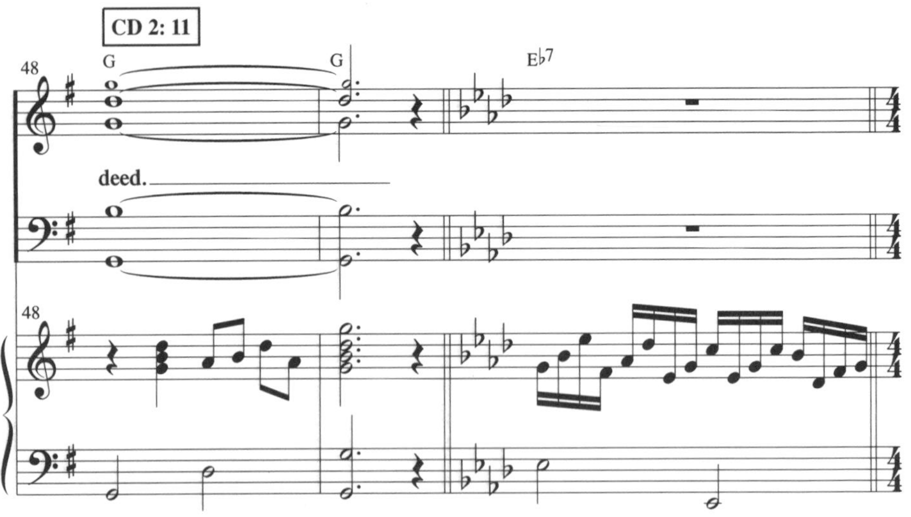

He Set Me Free

A.E.B.

ALBERT E. BRUMLEY

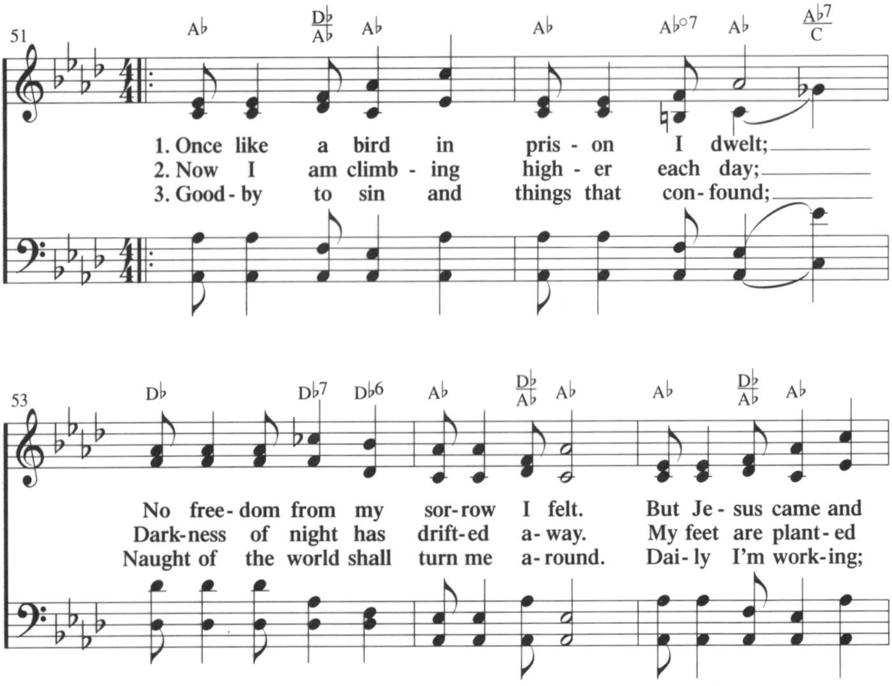
51
A♭ D♭/A♭ A♭ A♭ A♭°7 A♭ A♭7/C
1. Once like a bird in pris - on I dwelt;
2. Now I am climb - ing high - er each day;
3. Good - by to sin and things that con - found;
53
D♭ D♭7 D♭6 A♭ D♭/A♭ A♭ A♭ D♭/A♭ A♭
No free - dom from my sor - row I felt. But Je - sus came and
Dark - ness of night has drift - ed a - way. My feet are plant - ed
Naught of the world shall turn me a - round. Dai - ly I'm work - ing;

56
Ab Abo7 Ab Ab Ab/Eb Ab/C Ab Ab/Eb Eb7 Db/Eb Ab
lis- tened to me, And glo- ry to God, He set me free!
on high- er ground, And glo- ry to God, I'm home - ward bound!
I'm pray- ing, too, And glo- ry to God, I'm go - ing thro'.
CHORUS
59
Db Db7 Db7/F Ab Ab/Eb Ab6/C Ab Ab Db/Ab Ab
He set me free; He set me free. He broke the bonds of
yes, And
CD 2:12
1st time
62
Bb9 Bb7 Bb9/D Eb Ab Ab/Eb Ab/C Ab Ab7/C Db Ab
pris- on for me. I'm glo - ry- bound- my Je- sus to see, For,
65
Ab Ab/Eb Ab6/C Ab
1-2
Ab/Eb Eb7 Db/Eb Ab
3 Song Ending
Ab/Eb Eb7 Db/Eb Ab
glo- ry to God, He set me free. set me free.

3 Medley Ending
Ab/Eb Eb7 Db/Eb Ab
Ab
Fm/Ab Ab
set me free. He whom the Son sets free,
3 Medley Ending
Ab
Fm/Ab Ab
Ab/Eb Ab Cm7/G
He whom the Son sets free, He whom the
Fm Fm7 Fm Bb9
DbM7/Eb Eb7 Ab Ab
Son sets free is free, free in - deed.
End of Medley

SWEET BEULAH LAND Medley

SWEET BEULAH LAND
VERSE 1: SATB
CHORUS: SATB
VERSE 2: ladies unison through "...to labor;"; remainder of verse, SATB
CHORUS: SATB; medley ending

Arr. by Joseph Linn

(JESUS WILL BE WHAT MAKES IT) HEAVEN FOR ME
VERSE 1: SATB (basses sing melody)
CHORUS: SATB; medley ending

Sweet Beulah Land

S.P., Jr.

SQUIRE PARSONS, Jr.

CD 2:14 1st time
CD 2:16 2nd time
G Bm CM9 CM7 D7 Bm/D G G
For time won't mat - ter an - y - more.
Then I will take my heav'n-ly flight.
time won't mat - ter
I will take
CHORUS
G G G C/G G Am/G G G Am/G G G
Beu - lah Land, I'm long - ing for you; And some-
G G C/G G Am/G G Am add 11 D7 D13 D7
day on thee I'll stand. There my
G G C/G G Am/G G G B/F♯ B7/F♯ Em Em7
home shall be e - ter - nal– Beu - lah
CD 2:15 1st time
G/D Gsus/D C/D G/D Bm/D D7
1 G G
2 Song Ending G G
Land, sweet Beu - lah Land.
Land.

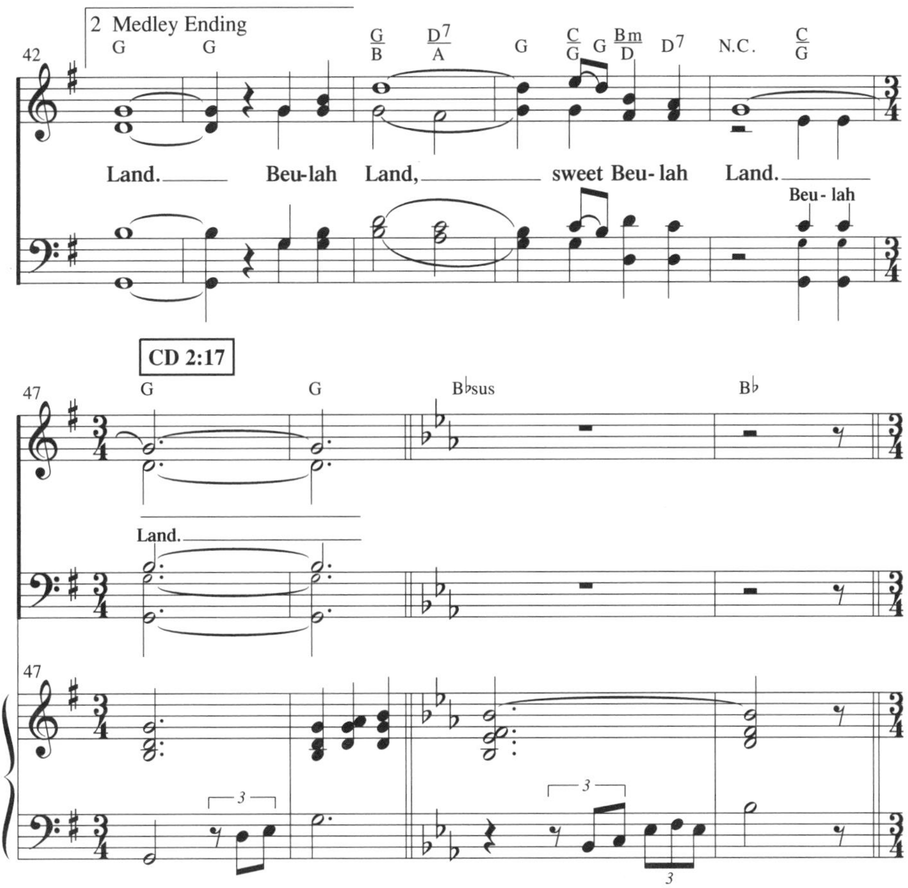

2 Medley Ending
42
G G G/B D7/A G C/G G Bm/D D7 N.C. C/G
Land. Beu-lah Land, sweet Beu-lah Land.
Beu-lah
CD 2:17
47
G G B♭sus B♭
Land.
47
3
3
3

(Jesus Will Be What Makes It) Heaven for Me

L.W. LANNY WOLFE

51
B♭sus/E♭ E♭ E♭7 E♭9 E♭7 Fm/A♭ A♭ Fm/A♭ E♭
1. I've heard of a land that is won-drous - ly fair; They
2. If walls there weren't jas - per, if streets were not gold, If

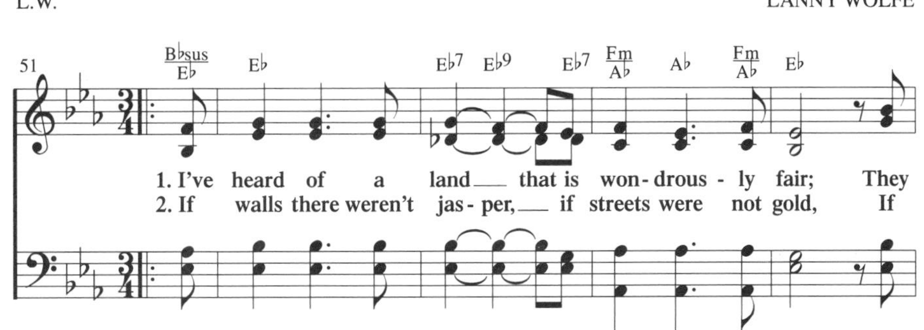

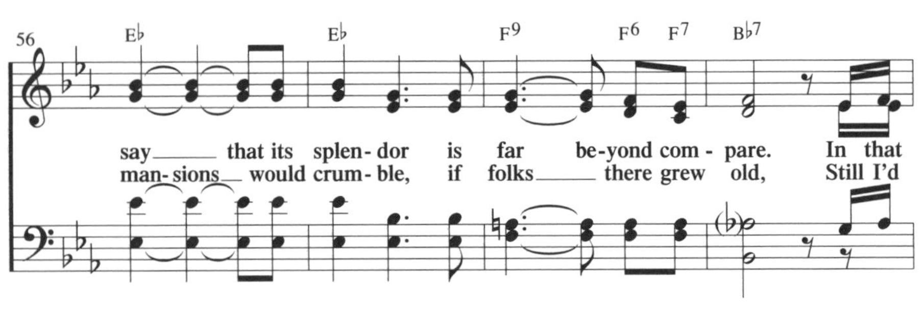
56
E♭ E♭ F9 F6 F7 B♭7
say___ that its splen- dor is far be-yond com - pare. In that
man- sions___ would crum- ble, if folks___ there grew old, Still I'd

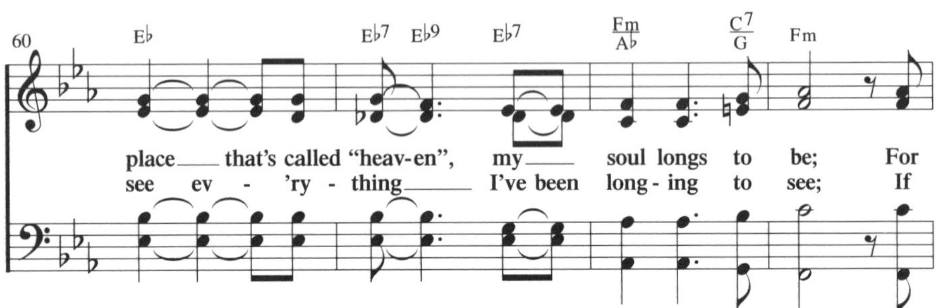
60
E♭ E♭7 E♭9 E♭7 Fm/A♭ C7/G Fm
place___ that's called "heav-en", my___ soul longs to be; For
see ev - 'ry - thing___ I've been long - ing to see; If

CD 2:18
64
Fm Gm Fm/A♭ E♭/B♭ B♭9 Gm/B♭ B♭7 E♭
where Je - sus is,___ it will be heav - en for me.
Je - sus is there,___ it will be heav - en for me.

CHORUS
68
A♭ B♭m/A♭ A♭ A♭/E♭ E♭ E♭ E♭
Heav - en for me, heav - en for me– Je - sus will

73
E♭ Cm/E♭ Cm7♯ Cm7 F9 F6 F7 B♭7 A♭/B♭ B♭7 E♭
be what makes it heav-en for me. All its beau-ty and
77
E♭7 E♭9 E♭7 Fm/A♭ C7/G Fm E♭/F Fm7 Gm Fm/A♭
won-ders I'm long-ing to see; But Je - sus will
81
E♭/B♭ Cm7 Fm7 Gm/B♭ B♭7
1 E♭
2 Song Ending E♭
be what makes it heav-en for me. me.
85
2 Medley Ending
E♭ Fm7 Gm Fm/A♭ E♭/B♭ E♭M7/B♭ G°7/B♭ G°7 Fm Gm/B♭ B♭7
me. Je - sus will be what makes it heav - en for
90
E♭/B♭ A♭M9 A♭ A♭m6 E♭ E♭
makes it heav - en, rit. (7)
me, heav - en for me.
End of Medley

HARD TRIALS Medley

Arr. by Joseph Linn

WE'LL SOON BE DONE WITH TROUBLES AND TRIALS
VERSE 1: SATB
CHORUS: SATB
VERSE 2: 1st phrase, ladies unison;
2nd phrase, SATB;
3rd phrase, ladies unison;
4th phrase, SATB
CHORUS: SATB; medley ending

HARD TRIALS WILL SOON BE OVER
VERSE 1: SATB
CHORUS: SATB
VERSE 2: SATB
CHORUS: SATB; medley ending

We'll Soon Be Done with Troubles and Trials

C.D. **CD 2:19** CLEAVANT DERRICKS

G/D D Dsus/E D D9/C G/B Am7 G
tri - als.
Safe from heart-ache, pain and
tri - als, trou-bles and tri - als.
'Tis a home of life so
Oh, what peace and joy sub -
G G9/B C G
care, we shall all that glo - ry share,
fair, and we'll all be gath-ered there,
lime in that home of love di - vine,
And I'm gon - na
G/D Am/G G G/D D7
Sit down be-side my Je - sus,
Lord, I'm gon-na
sit down and rest a lit-tle
CHORUS
G G N.C. G G
while.
We'll soon be done
We'll soon be done with trou-bles and

27
Am/G G N.C. D7 D7 Bm/D D7
tri - als, yes, in that home on the oth - er
trou - bles and tri - als, In that home,
31
G N.C. C
side. Shake glad hands with the
on the oth - er side, And I'm a gon - na
34
Am/C C G C/G G N.C.
eld - ers, tell my kin - dred good morn - ing,
Lord, and Then I'm gon - na
CD 2:20 1st time
CD 2:21 2nd time
37
G/D Am/D G/D Em Cm6/E♭ G/D D9
Sit down be - side my Je - sus, gon - na sit down and rest a lit - tle
Lord, I'm
40
1,2
G G
3 Song Ending
G G G/B D G rit. G/D D7
while. while. Gon - na sit down and rest a lit - tle

3 Medley Ending
45
G G7 C/G Cm/G G G G G
while.
while, gon-na rest a lit-tle while.
while.

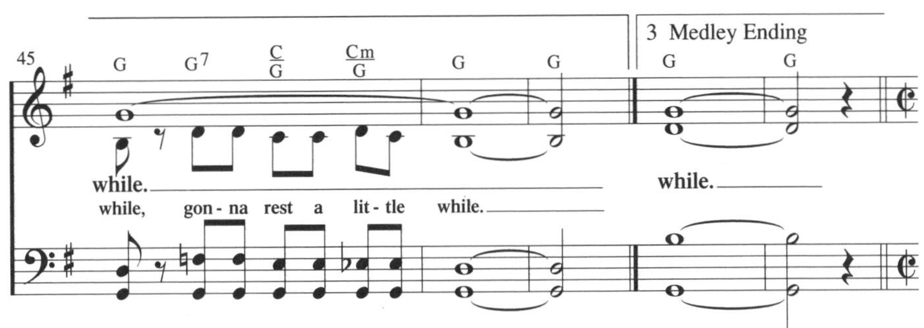

Hard Trials Will Soon Be Over

M.L. MOSIE LISTER

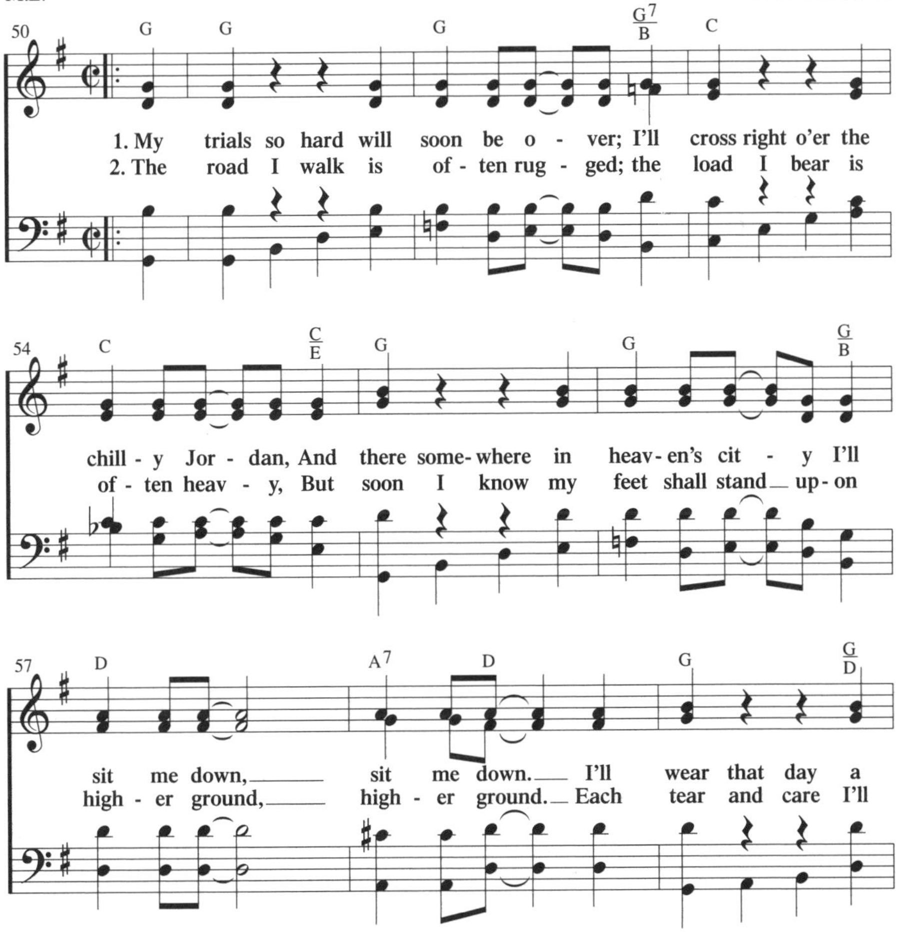

50
G G G G7/B C
1. My trials so hard will soon be o - ver; I'll cross right o'er the
2. The road I walk is of - ten rug - ged; the load I bear is
54
C C/E G G G/B
chill - y Jor - dan, And there some-where in heav-en's cit - y I'll
of - ten heav - y, But soon I know my feet shall stand up-on
57
D A7 D G G/D
sit me down, sit me down. I'll wear that day a
high - er ground, high - er ground. Each tear and care I'll

60
B7
Em
B7/F♯
crown of glo - ry; I'll shout and tell the hap - py sto - ry. My
leave be - hind me; I'll shout and say good - by to trou - ble. My
CD 2:22
63
Em
A9
A9/E
A7
G/D
D7
G
hard trials will soon be o - ver and I shall wear a crown.
hard trials will soon be o - ver and I shall wear a crown.
CHORUS
67
N.C.
C
C
G
Lord, I'm tired, so tired.
Hard trials will soon be o - ver, Hard trials will
71
G
G
G
D
D/F♯
A7/E
A7
Soon my Lord's gon-na come for me; then I'll be heav-en -
soon be o - ver.
75
D
N.C.
C
C
G
bound. Then I'll fly to the sky.
Hard trials will soon be o - ver, Hard trials will

79
G
Em
A9
A9/E
A7
G/D
D7
Hard trials will soon be o - ver and I shall wear a
soon be o - ver.
83
1
G
G
crown.
2 Song Ending
G
G
crown.
2 Medley Ending
G
G
crown.
89
Em
A9
A9/E
A7
G/D
D7sus
D7
Hard trials will soon be o - ver and I shall wear a
My
93
G
G
N.C.
G/B
D7/A
G
crown.
I shall wear a crown.
trials so hard will soon be o - ver and
End of Medley

GREAT GRACE Medley

Arr. by Joseph Linn

ALL BECAUSE OF GOD'S AMAZING GRACE
VERSE 1: ladies unison
CHORUS: SATB; medley ending

ALL IN THE NAME OF JESUS
VERSE 1: 1st half, SAT;
unison through "...forgiveness too,";
remainder of verse, SATB
CHORUS: SATB
VERSE 2: 1st phrase, ladies unison;
2nd phrase, men unison;
all unison through "...friendship true,";
remainder of verse, SATB
CHORUS: SATB; medley ending

All Because of God's Amazing Grace

CD 2:24

hold
C7 C7/E F G/F F F#°7 C/G
lost, yet now I'm found; tho' I was blind-ed,
guid - ed safe - ly through, and it will sure - ly
mer - cy for sin did a - tone; thro' count-less a - ges this
CHORUS (With a shuffle feel)
Am6 G7 C C G7 C Dm7 C7/E F
now I see!
lead us home!
song we'll sing:
(1,2.) And it's
(3.) It was
all be-cause of God's a-maz-ing
C G7/D C G/B Am Am7 D7 Bm/D D7
grace– be-cause on Cal-v'ry's moun-tain He took my
Dm/G Dm7/G G C Gm7 C7/G C7
place! And Oh, some-day, some glo-rious morn-ing I shall

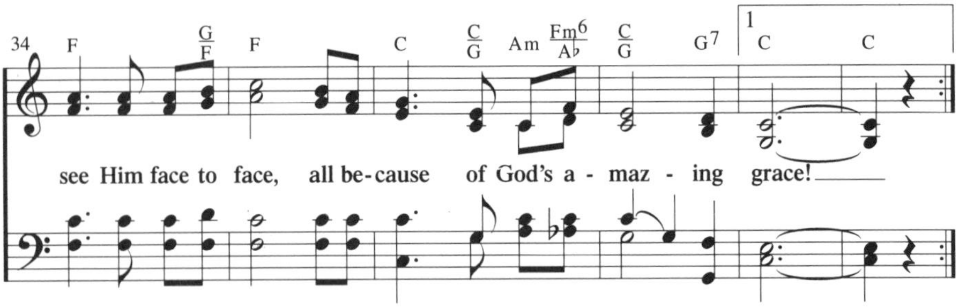
34
F
G
F
F
C
C
G
Am
Fm6
A♭
C
G
G7
1
C
C
see Him face to face, all be-cause of God's a - maz - ing grace!

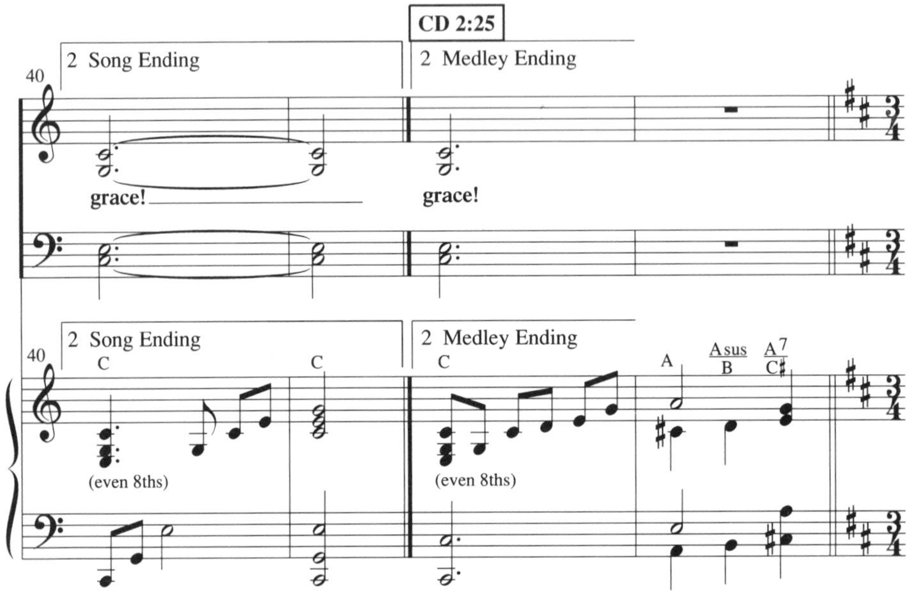
CD 2:25
40
2 Song Ending
2 Medley Ending
grace!
grace!
40
2 Song Ending
C
C
2 Medley Ending
C
A
Asus
B
A7
C♯
(even 8ths)
(even 8ths)

All in the Name of Jesus

S.R.A. STEPHEN R. ADAMS

44
D
DM7
D6
D
1. Truth and beau - ty and hap - pi - ness– it's
2. Care and com - fort, heal-ing and grace– it's

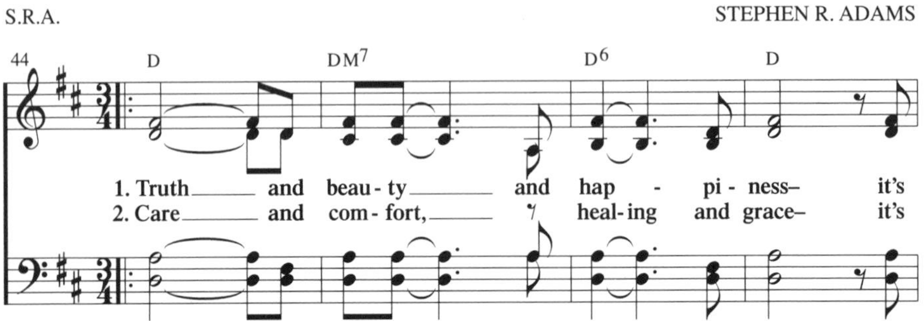

48
D
Am6 / C
B+
B7
Em9
Em
Em7
A7
all in the name of Je - sus.
all in the name of Je - sus.
52
Em
Em7♯
Em7
A9
Health and heav-en, peace and rest– it's
Wel-come, par-don, a hid - ing place–
56
Em7
G♯ / E
A
G / A
G / D
D
D
D
all in the name of Je - sus. Joy and
all in the name of Je - sus. Warmth and
61
DM7
D6
D
D
glad - ness, for - give - ness too, life ev - er -
sun - shine, friend - ship true, ful - fill-ment and

65
D Em7 D7/F♯ G G G GM7 G♯°7 C♯/G♯ G♯°7
last - ing and free, All that I've longed for and
bless - ing un - told, Hope for to - mor - row and
CD 2:26 1st time
CD 2:28 2nd time
70
D/A Bm Bm7 Em Em7 F♯m/A A7
all I need– it's all in the name of
help for to - day– it's all in the name of
74
Em/D D D A7sus/E D/F♯ CHORUS G GM7 Em6/G F♯m F♯m7 Bm
Je - sus.
Je - sus.
Je - sus, Je - sus– He's
80
Em7 A7 A/C♯ A7/C♯ D D Em7 D7/F♯ G GM7
here and He will show you the way. Oh, Je -

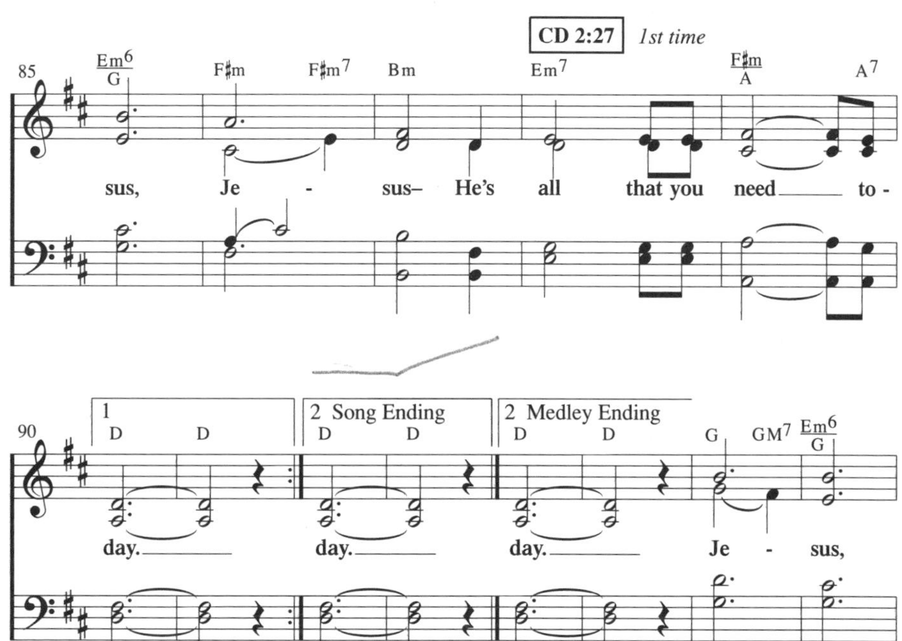

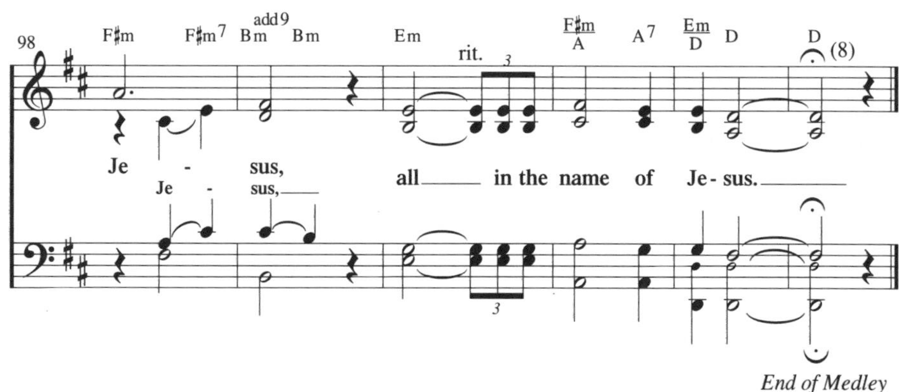

End of Medley

My God Is Real

K.M.

VERSE 1: solo, with ATB background vocals
CHORUS: solo, with SATB background vocals
VERSE 3: solo, with ATB background vocals
CHORUS: solo, with SATB background vocals; extended choral ending

KENNETH MORRIS
Arr. by Joseph Linn

CD 2:30 1st time
CD 2:32 2nd time
thing– That God is real, for I can feel Him deep with- in.
part– And God is real, for I can feel Him in my heart.
hour, God has been real, for I can feel His ho - ly pow'r.
of this one thing– real, for I can feel Him deep with- in, deep with- in.
I'll take God's part– real, for I can feel Him in my heart, in my heart.
yes, since that hour, real, for I can feel His ho - ly pow'r, ho- ly pow'r.
Him deep with- in.
Him in my heart.
His ho - ly pow'r.
CHORUS
My God is real, real in my soul. My God is
My God is real, real in my soul.
real, for He has washed and made me whole. His love for
real, for He has washed and made me whole, made me whole.

CD 2:31
1st time
19
G G7 C C6 C♯°7 G/D D7
me is like pure gold. My God is real, for I can feel Him in my
His love for me is like pure gold. real, feel
22
1,2
3 Song Ending
3 Extended Choral Ending
G C/G G G C/G G G C/G G C♯°7
soul. soul. soul. My God is
Him in my soul. Him in my soul. soul, in my soul.
25
G/D D7 C7 G C♯°7 G/D D7
real, for I can feel Him in my soul. My God is real, for I can feel Him in my
real, I can feel Him down in my soul. real, I can feel Him

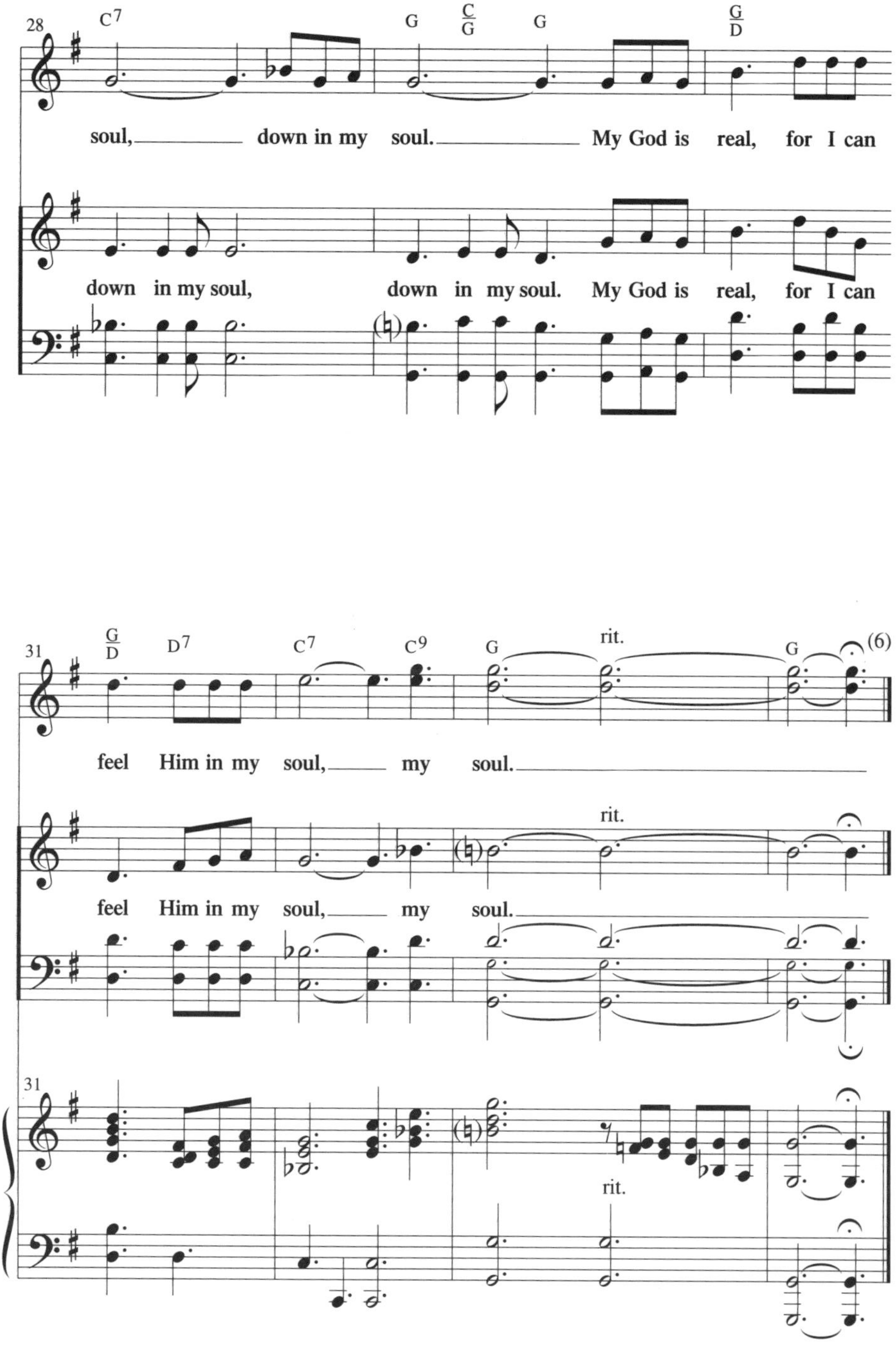

31
G/D D7 C7 C9 G rit. G (6)

feel Him in my soul, my soul.

rit.

feel Him in my soul, my soul.

31

rit.

God Bless the U.S.A.

L.G.

VERSE 1: solo
CHORUS: SATB
VERSE 2: 1st phrase, men unison;
2nd phrase, ladies unison;
3rd phrase, solo;
4th phrase, unison
CHORUS: SATB; extended choral ending

LEE GREENWOOD
Arr. by Joseph Linn

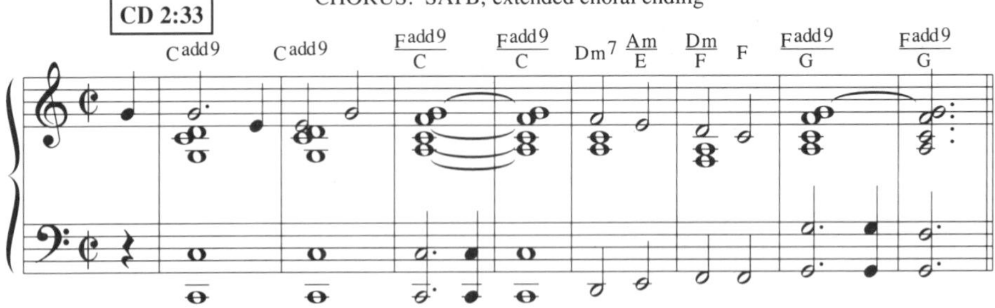

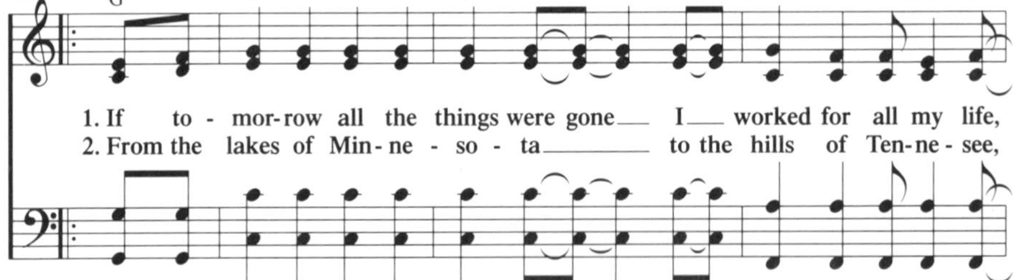

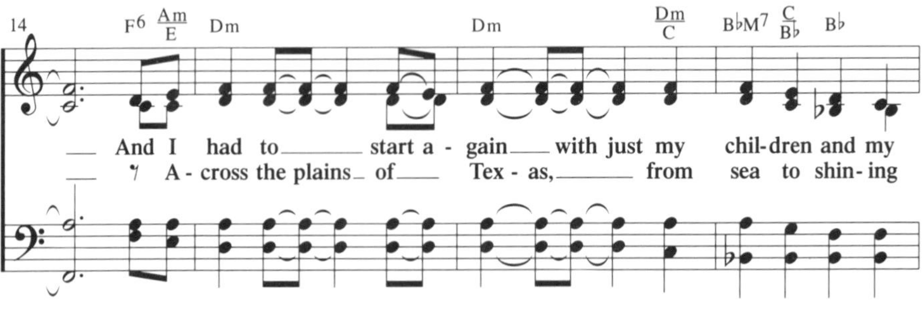

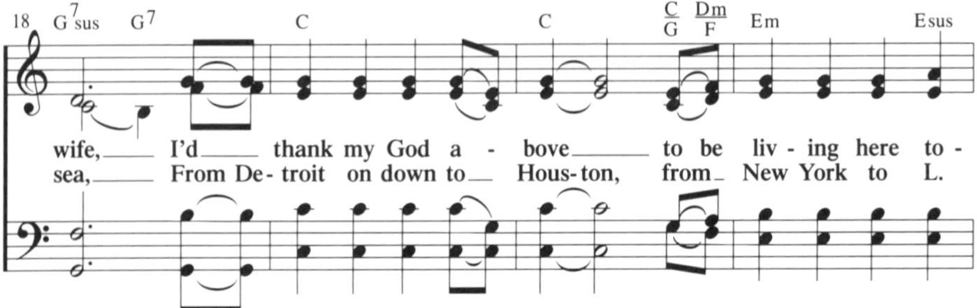

CD 2:34 1st time
CD 2:36 2nd time
Em Em7 Em Dm Dm
day, 'Cause the flag still stands for free - dom, and they
A., There's pride in ev - 'ry A - mer - i - can heart, and it's
Am Am7 Am Am/G F
CHORUS
N.C. G
can't take that a - way! And I'm
time we stand and say: That I'm proud to be an A -
G F/G F C N.C. G
mer - i - can where at least I know I'm free; And I won't for - get the
G F/G F C Am/C Em7/B Am
men who died, who gave that right to me. And I'd glad - ly stand up
Cadd9/E C/E F Fadd9 F C N.C. F Dm Csus/D
next to you and de - fend her still to - day, 'Cause there ain't no doubt I

CD 2:35
42
love this land! God bless the U. S. A.
47
2 Song Ending
bless the U. S. A.
2 Extended Choral Ending
54
bless the U. S. A. And I'd glad-ly stand up next to you and de-
58
fend her still to - day, 'Cause there ain't no doubt I love this land! God
63
bless the U. S. A. God bless the U. S. A.

Rise and Be Healed

M.B.

MILTON BOURGEOIS

Arr. by Joseph Linn

VERSE 1: 1st half, unison;
2nd half, SATB (basses sing melody)
CHORUS: SATB
VERSE 2: 1st half, ladies unison;
3rd phrase, men unison;
4th phrase, all unison
CHORUS: SATB; extended choral ending

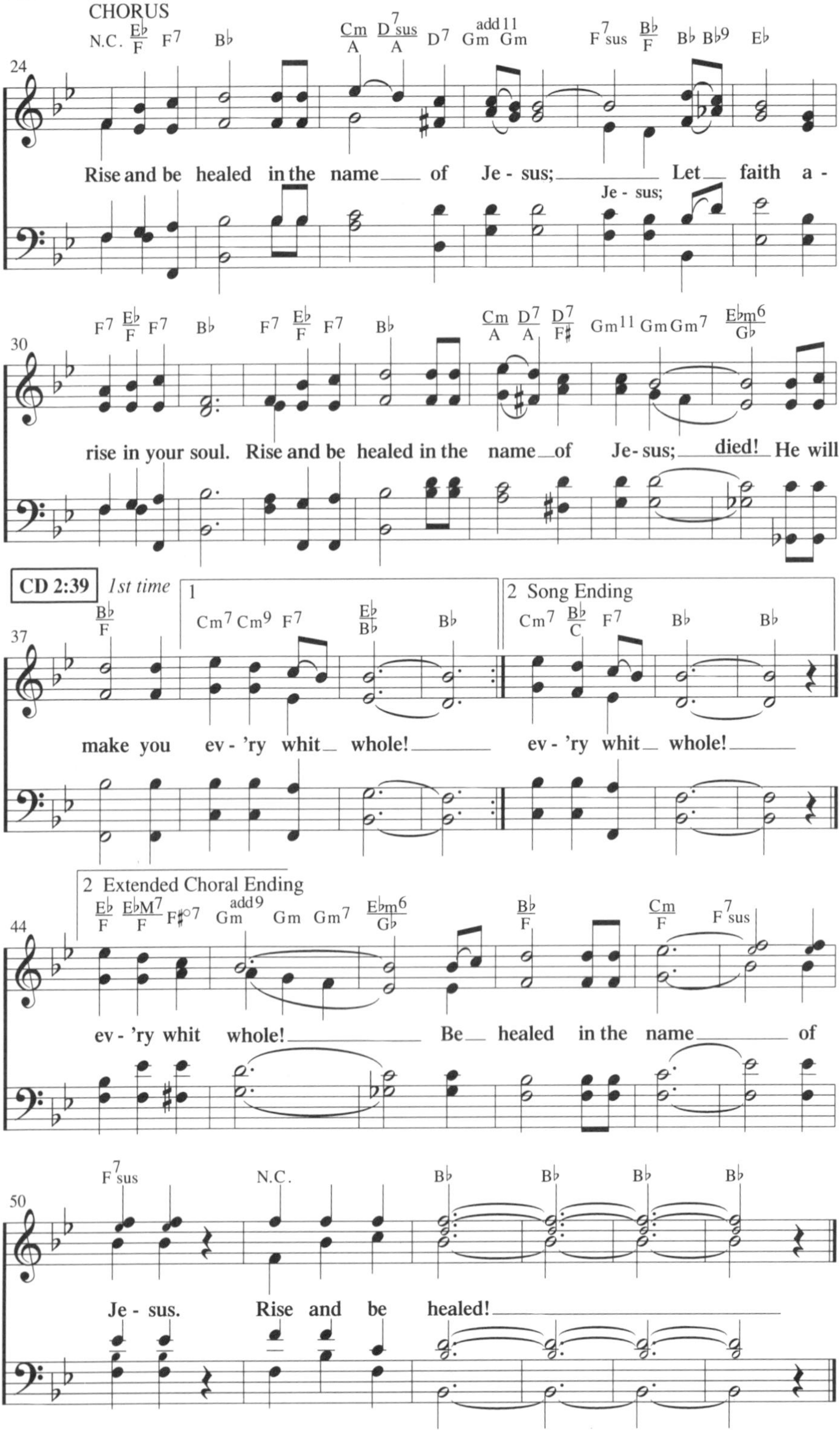
CHORUS
N.C. Eb/F F7 Bb Cm/A D7sus/A D7 Gm add11 Gm F7sus Bb/F Bb Bb9 Eb
Rise and be healed in the name of Je - sus; Let faith a -
Je - sus;
F7 Eb/F F7 Bb F7 Eb/F F7 Bb Cm/A D7/A D7/F# Gm11 Gm Gm7 Ebm6/Gb
rise in your soul. Rise and be healed in the name of Je - sus; died! He will
CD 2:39
1st time
1
2 Song Ending
Bb/F Cm7 Cm9 F7 Eb/Bb Bb Cm7 Bb/C F7 Bb Bb
make you ev - 'ry whit whole! ev - 'ry whit whole!
2 Extended Choral Ending
Eb/F EbM7/F F#o7 Gm add9 Gm Gm7 Ebm6/Gb Bb/F Cm/F F7sus
ev - 'ry whit whole! Be healed in the name of
F7sus N.C. Bb Bb Bb Bb
Je - sus. Rise and be healed!

I'LL PRAISE HIM Medley

FROM THE FIRST HALLELUJAH TO THE LAST AMEN
VERSE 1: SATB
CHORUS: SATB
VERSE 2: unison through "...together now to"; SATB on "praise the Lord."
CHORUS: SATB; medley ending

Arr. by Joseph Linn

THE ROCKS SHALL NOT CRY OUT
CHORUS: SATB
VERSE 1: SATB
CHORUS: SATB; coda

From the First Hallelujah to the Last Amen

D.B. DAVE BOLLING

10
G
G/B
D
G
old camp-meet-ings on the grass or tem-ples built by men, A
if you feel re-strict-ed, strike a brand new chord. Let's
you can't praise the Sav-ior now, you'll be em-bar-rassed then When
12
G
C/G
Em7
Cm/E♭
Cm6/E♭
G/D
D7
G
CHORUS
N.C.
saint shouts hal-le-lu-jah and we all join in.
all a-gree to-geth-er now to praise the Lord. From the
we sing hal-le-lu-jah and the an-gels say a-men.
16
G
G
D7
G
G
C/G
G
Am/G
G
first hal-le-lu-jah to the last a-men, I'll praise the Lord and then I'll
19
A7
D7
G
Am/G
G
Am/G
G
Am/G
G
D7
G
praise Him a-gain– Shar-ing the love of Je-sus with all men From the

CD 2:42
1st time
1,2
3 Song Ending
22
G
C/G
G
Em
Cm6/E♭
G/D
D7
G
first hal - le- lu- jah to the last a - men. last a - men.
3 Medley Ending
27
D7sus
N.C.
C
G/B
last a - men, a -
a - men, a - men
CD 2:43
30
men.

The Rocks Shall Not Cry Out

D.W. and R.M. DARYL WILLIAMS and RICH MOORE

End of Medley

HE CAME TO ME Medley

Arr. by Joseph Linn

HE CAME TO ME
VERSE 1: SATB
CHORUS: SATB; medley ending

THE GENTLE STRANGER
VERSE 1: ladies unison
CHORUS: SATB
VERSE 2: SAT
CHORUS: SATB; medley ending

He Came to Me

S.P., Jr. SQUIRE PARSONS, Jr.

13
D D D/C G/B Am7 D7 C/D Bm/D D7
ford. From where I was, to His de-mand– it seemed so
in. He picked me up and drew me gent - ly to His
CD 2:46
17
G G Bm Bm/A E7/G♯ Bm/F♯ E7 Bm7 C♯m/E E7
far. I cried, "Dear Lord, I can - not come to where You
side Where to - day in His sweet love I now a -
CHORUS
21
G/A A7 G/A A7 A7/C♯ D F♯m/E D7 Am/E D7/F♯
are." He came to me; He came to
bide.
me, He came to me, He came to
26
G B7/F♯ Em Em7 A Em7 Em A G/A A7 A9
me. When I could not come to where He was, He came to
me, came to me,

30 D D/F♯ D/A A A7/C♯ D F♯m/E D7 Am/E D7/F♯

me.______ That's why He died ______ on Cal - va -
He came to me. why He died, that's why He died on Cal - va -

CD 2:47

34 G B7/F♯ Em Em7 A Em7 Em A G/A A7

ry– ______ When I could not come to where He was, He came to
ry, Cal - va - ry.

38 1 D D | 2 Song Ending D D | 2 Medley Ending D B♭sus

me.______ me.______ me.

The Gentle Stranger

M.L. MOSIE LISTER

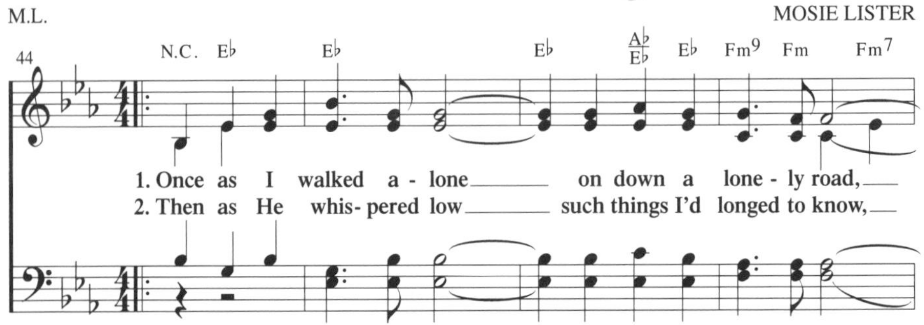

48
B♭7
E♭/B♭
B♭9
A♭/B♭
Gm/B♭
Fm7/B♭
A♭/B♭
Gm/B♭
D/B♭
E♭
And had no one to bear my sor-row or my blame,
My heart re-joiced to know the won-der of His grace.
52
E♭
E♭
E♭
A♭/E♭
E♭
Fm9
Fm
Fm7
A gen-tle Stran-ger came and took me by the hand,
I've learned to love Him so, and this I sure-ly know–
CD 2:48
1st time
CD 2:50
2nd time
56
B♭7
E♭/B♭
B♭9
A♭/B♭
Gm/B♭
B♭9
Fm7
Fm9
Gm/B♭
B♭7
E♭
E♭
And some-how ev-'ry care de-part-ed when He came.
He'll be no stran-ger when I see Him face to face.
CHORUS
61
E♭
E♭7
A♭
A♭
A♭/E♭
E♭
So filled with won-der, my heart still thrills to know
65
E♭
A♭/E♭
E♭
E♭/B♭
Fm/B♭
Fm/B♭
A♭/B♭
Gm/B♭
D/B♭
E♭
E♭
E♭7
The gen-tle Stran-ger who loves me so. My Lord for-

70
A♭ A♭ A♭/E♭ E♭ E♭ A♭/E♭ E♭
ev - er, my King He'll al - ways be– The gen - tle
CD 2:49
1st time
74
Fm9 Fm Fm Fm7 Gm/B♭ B♭7
1 E♭ E♭
2 Song Ending E♭ E♭
Stran - ger from Gal - i - lee. lee.
80
2 Medley Ending
lee. The gen - tle Stran - ger
80
2 Medley Ending
E♭ E♭ A♭/E♭ E♭ F9sus Fm7
8va
83
rit.
(9)
from Gal - i - lee.
83
B♭7 A♭/B♭ Gm/B♭ B♭7 E♭
rit.
End of Medley

This Ole House

VERSE 1: solo
CHORUS: SATB
VERSE 2: solo
CHORUS: SATB
VERSE 3: solo
CHORUS: SATB
VERSE 4: solo
CHORUS: SATB; extended choral ending

STUART HAMBLEN
Arr. by Joseph Linn

S.H.

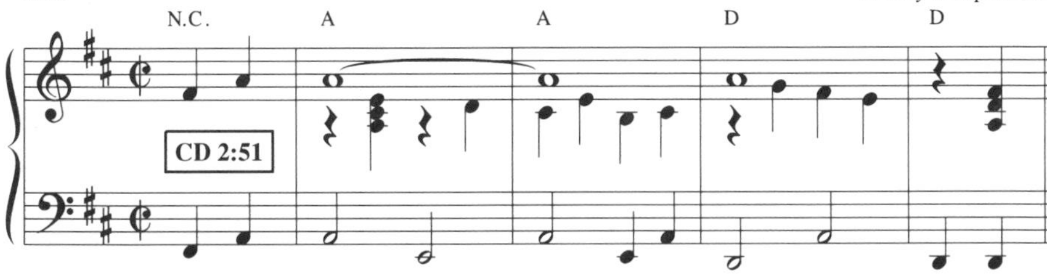

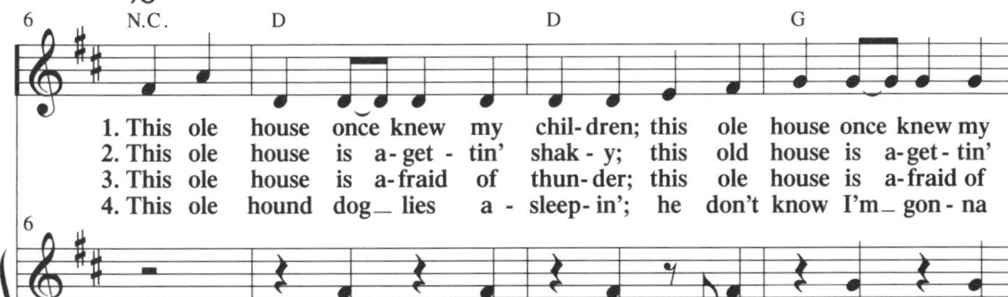

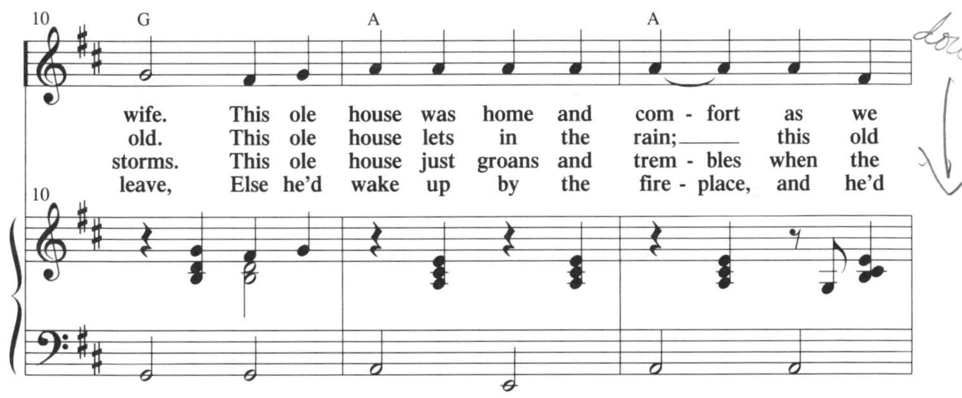

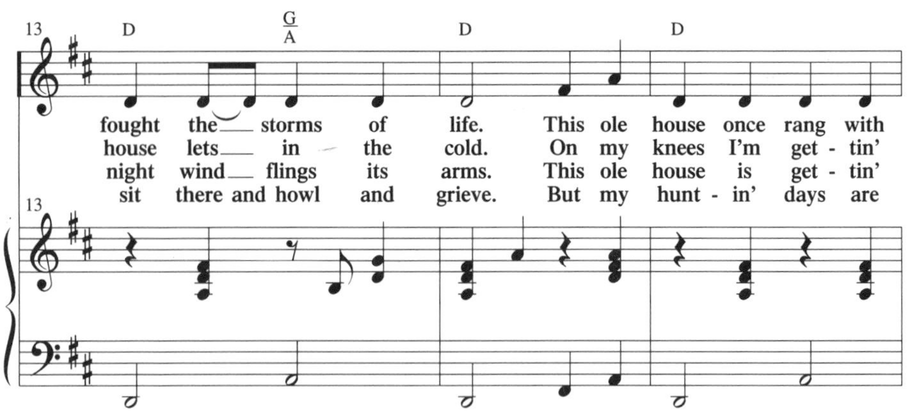

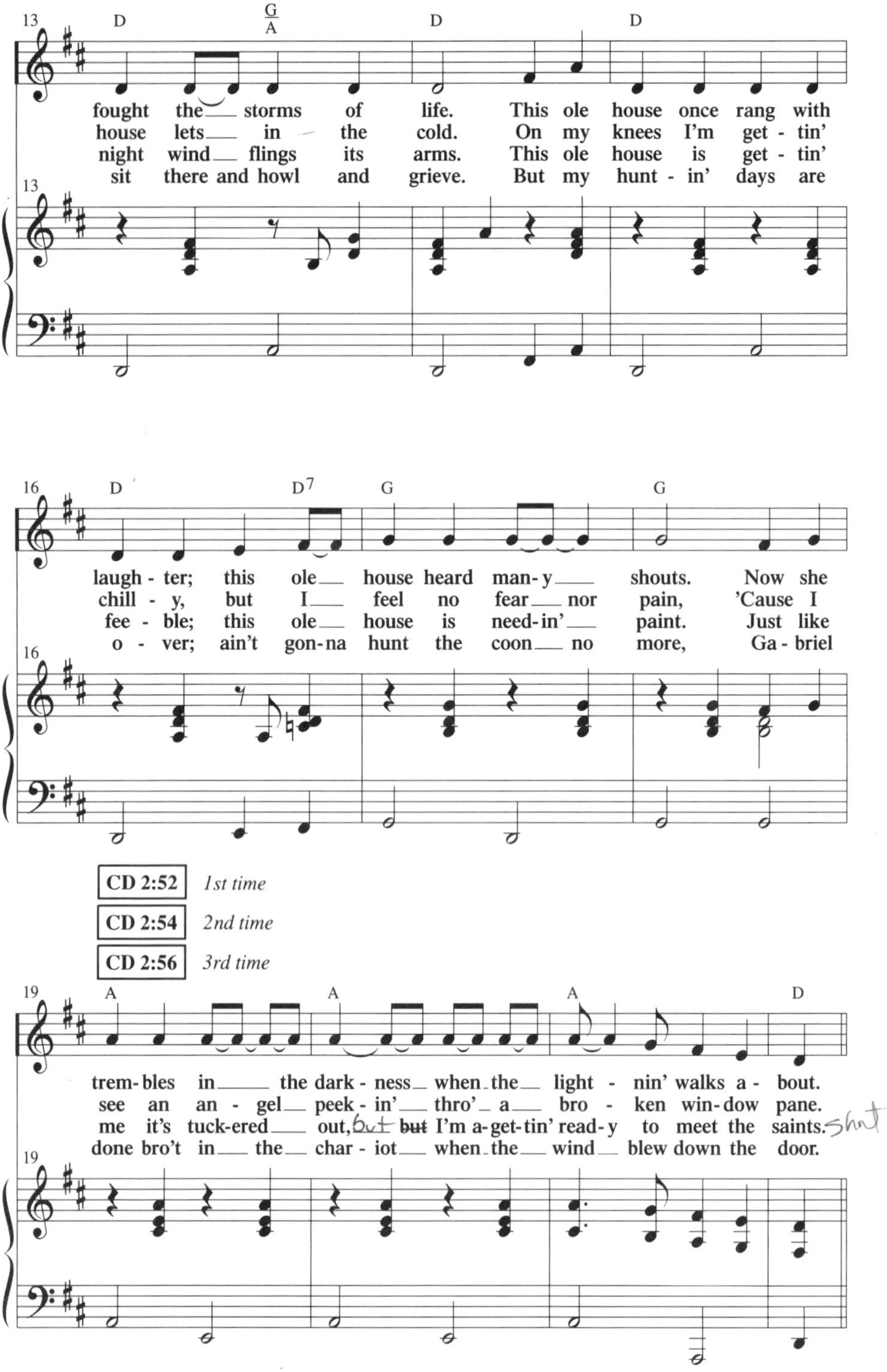
13
D
G/A
D
D
fought the storms of life. This ole house once rang with
house lets in the cold. On my knees I'm get - tin'
night wind flings its arms. This ole house is get - tin'
sit there and howl and grieve. But my hunt - in' days are
16
D
D7
G
G
laugh - ter; this ole house heard man - y shouts. Now she
chill - y, but I feel no fear nor pain, 'Cause I
fee - ble; this ole house is need - in' paint. Just like
o - ver; ain't gon - na hunt the coon no more, Ga - briel
CD 2:52 1st time
CD 2:54 2nd time
CD 2:56 3rd time
19
A
A
A
D
trem - bles in the dark - ness when the light - nin' walks a - bout.
see an an - gel peek - in' thro' a bro - ken win - dow pane.
me it's tuck - ered out, but I'm a - get - tin' read - y to meet the saints.
done bro't in the char - iot when the wind blew down the door.

CHORUS
23
D
A/D
D7
G
G
Well, I ain't a - gon - na need this house no long - er; ain't a - gon - na
26
D
D
A
A
A7
need this house no more– Ain't got time to fix the shin - gles, ain't got
time,
30
D6
D
D7
G
G
time to fix the door, Ain't got time to oil the hing - es, nor to
time
34
Bm/D
D
D
A
mend the win - dow pane, Ain't a - gon - na need this house no

CD 2:53 1st time
CD 2:55 2nd time
1-3
37
A
A
A7
F♯m
A
A7
D
D
long- er. I'm a get-tin' read-y to meet the saints.
1-3
41
D.S.
4 Song Ending
D
saints.

4 Extended Choral Ending
47
D
D
A
saints. Ain't a - gon - na need this house no
50
A
A
A7
F♯m
A
A7
D
long - er. I'm a get-tin' read - y to meet the saints. I'm a get-tin'
B♭
D
53
C
D
read - y, get - tin' read - y to
59
meet the saints.

NEVER ALONE Medley

Arr. by Joseph Linn

WHERE NO ONE STANDS ALONE
VERSE 1: 1st half, unison;
2nd half, SATB (basses sing melody)
CHORUS: SATB; medley ending

HIS HAND IN MINE
VERSE 1: SA through "...always be.";
remainder of verse, SAT
CHORUS: SATB
VERSE 2: SAT
CHORUS: SATB; medley ending

Where No One Stands Alone

M.L. — MOSIE LISTER

CD 2:58
heart felt a - lone and I cried, "O Lord, don't hide Your
don't know a thing in this whole wide world that's worse than
face from me."
be - ing a - lone.
CHORUS
N.C.
Hold my hand, all the way, ev - 'ry
Hold my hand, all the way,
hour, ev - 'ry day, From here to the great un -
ev - 'ry hour, ev - 'ry day,
known. Take my hand; let me stand where
no one stands a - lone.
1
lone.
2 Song Ending
lone.

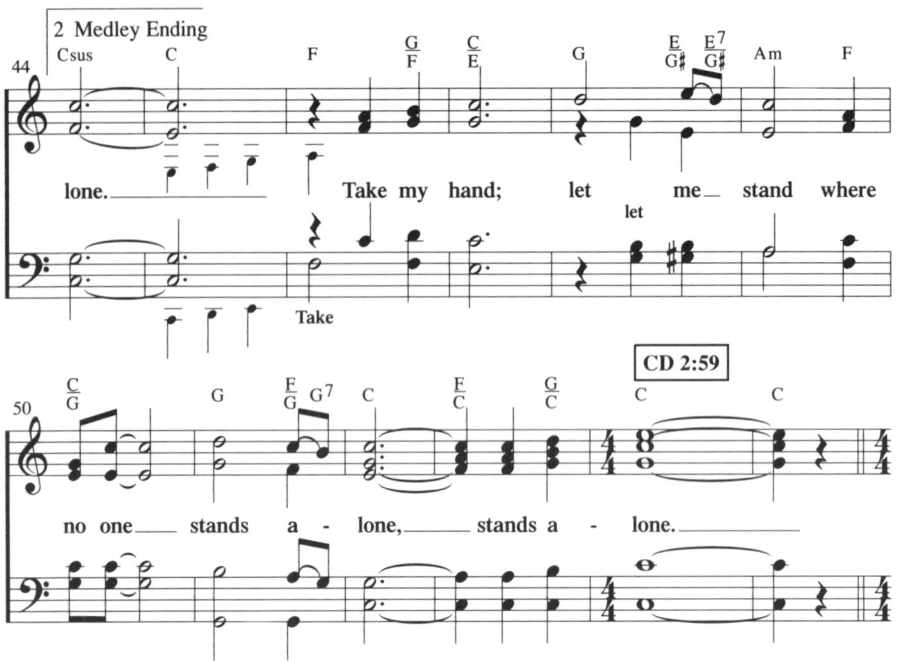

His Hand in Mine

M.L. MOSIE LISTER

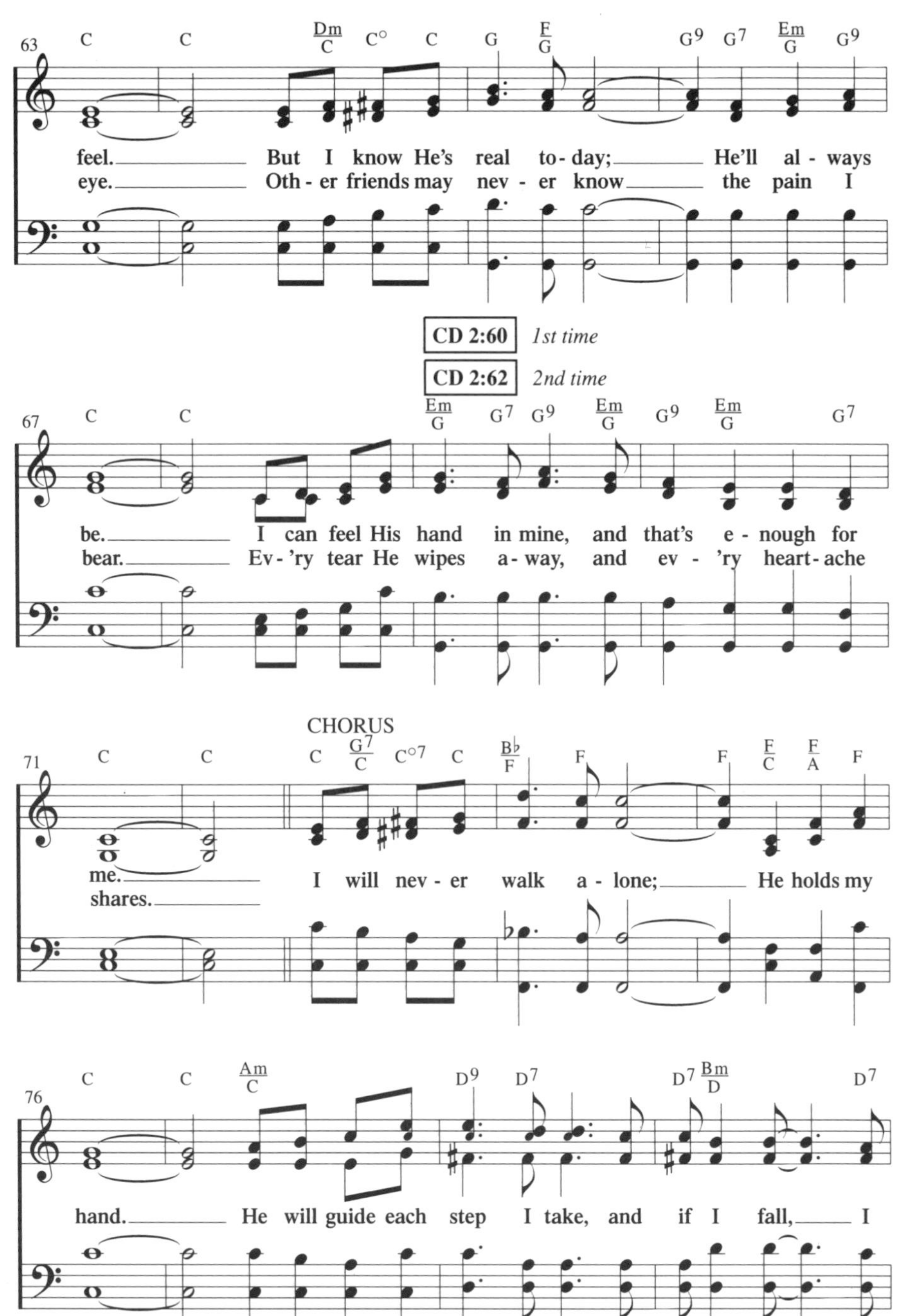
63
C C Dm/C C° C G F/G G9 G7 Em/G G9
feel. But I know He's real to-day; He'll al-ways
eye. Oth-er friends may nev-er know the pain I
CD 2:60 1st time
CD 2:62 2nd time
67
C C Em/G G7 G9 Em/G G9 Em/G G7
be. I can feel His hand in mine, and that's e-nough for
bear. Ev-'ry tear He wipes a-way, and ev-'ry heart-ache
CHORUS
71
C C C G7/C C°7 C B♭/F F F F/C F/A F
me. I will nev-er walk a-lone; He holds my
shares.
76
C C Am/C D9 D7 D7 Bm/D D7
hand. He will guide each step I take, and if I fall, I

know He'll un - der - stand. Till the day He tells me why He loves me
(alt. lyrics) When the time shall come to leave this world be -
CD 2:61
1st time
so, I can feel His hand in mine; that's all I need to
hind, I will walk that lone - some val - ley with His hand in
1
2 Song Ending
2 Medley Ending
know. know. know. I can feel His
mine. mine. mine.
hand in mine; that's all I need to know.
End of Medley

BELIEVE IT! Medley

Arr. by Joseph Linn

GOD SAID IT, I BELIEVE IT, THAT SETTLES IT
VERSE 1: unison
CHORUS: SATB
VERSE 2: 1st half, ladies unison; 2nd half, SAT
CHORUS: SATB; medley ending

IF YOU BELIEVE
CHORUS: SATB
VERSE 1: men unison
CHORUS: SATB
VERSE 3: men unison
CHORUS: SATB; coda

God Said It, I Believe It, That Settles It

S.R.A. and GENE BRAUN

STEPHEN R. ADAMS

CHORUS
mir-a-cle has hap-pened to me! God said it, and I be-
mir-a-cle can hap-pen to you.
lieve it, and that set-tles it for me! God
said it, and I be-lieve it, and that set-tles it for
me! Though some may doubt that His Word is true, I've
CD 2:64
1st time
cho-sen to be-lieve it; now, how a-bout you? God said it, and I be-

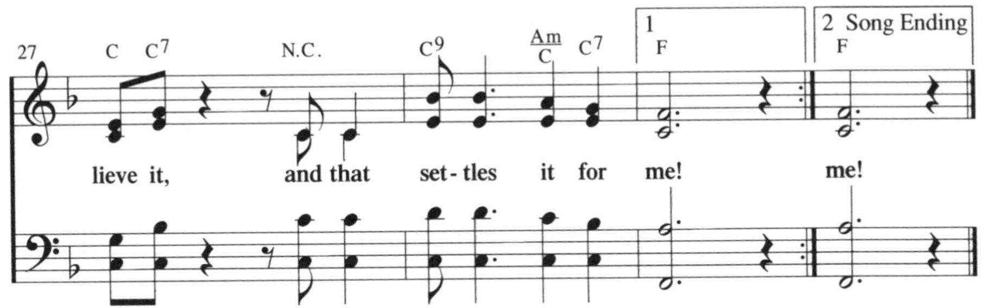

If You Believe

M.L.

MOSIE LISTER

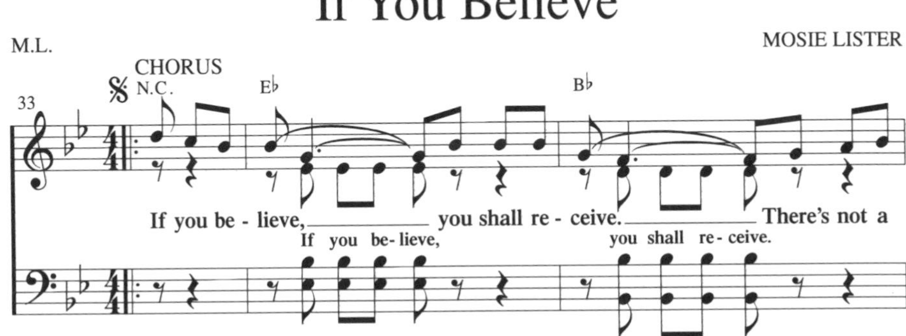

36
C
Csus
D
C
E
Am
C
C7
F7
Dm
F
trou-ble or care the good Lord can't re - lieve. Oh,
38
B♭
B♭sus
C
B♭
D
C7
He is just the same to-day; All you have to do is just
Medley: last time to Coda
40
F7
F9
F7
B♭
Fine
trust and pray, and be - lieve. You must be - lieve.
43
N.C.
B♭
E♭
B♭
B♭
F7
F9
F7
F9
1. I read a - bout how Paul and Si - las were in jail, And no one
2. When Dan-iel sat with-in the hun-gry li - on's den, No-bod-y
3. When Da-vid stood be-fore the gi - ant with his sling, Go-li-ath
(1) I read a - bout
46
F7
B♭
B♭°7
B♭
there, no - bod - y there could go their bail. But when they
thought that there was an - y hope for him. But all night
laughed at such a pu - ny lit - tle thing. But Da - vid
And no one there,

CD 2:66 1st time
CD 2:67 2nd time
prayed, they found that God was on their side; That jail-house
long, the li - ons nev - er took a bite; God took a -
knew his faith in God would stand the test. He flung the
But when they prayed
door swung o - pen wide.
way their ap - pe - tite.
rock; God did the rest.
That jail - house door
1,2
3 Song Ending D.S. al Fine
3 Medley Ending D.S. al Coda
CODA
Be - lieve, you must be - lieve. You must be -
rest. lieve. Be - lieve, you must be - lieve.
lieve, be - lieve.
You must be - lieve. You must be - lieve.
End of Medley

STORM Medley

'TIL THE STORM PASSES BY *Arr. by Joseph Linn*

VERSE 1: SATB
CHORUS: 1st half, unison;
2nd half, SATB
VERSE 3: 1st half, ladies unison;
2nd half, SATB
CHORUS: 1st half, unison;
2nd half, SATB; medley ending

PEACE IN THE MIDST OF THE STORM

CHORUS: SATB
VERSE 1: solo
CHORUS: SATB; coda

14
D A7sus/D D A7/E D/F♯ D Asus/E D/F♯ G
place. 'Mid the crash of the thun-der, pre-cious Lord, hear my
by." But I know Thou art with me, and to-mor-row I'll
shore. In that land where the tem-pest nev-er comes, Lord, may
CD 2:69 1st time
CD 2:71 2nd time
18
G D/A Bm6 E7/B D/A A7 D D
cry; Keep me safe 'til the storm pass-es by.
rise Where the storms nev-er dark-en the skies.
I Dwell with Thee when the storm pass-es by.
CHORUS
23
D A D/A A7 F♯m/A A7 D D D/F♯
'Til the storm pass-es o-ver, 'til the thun-der sounds no more, 'Til the
28
E7 E7 F♯m/E E7 A A7 D
clouds roll for-ev-er from the sky, Hold me fast, let me
CD 2:70 1st time
33
D D7/F♯ Em/G G D G D Bm6 Gm6/B♭ D/A A7
stand in the hol-low of Thy hand. Keep me safe 'til the storm pass-es

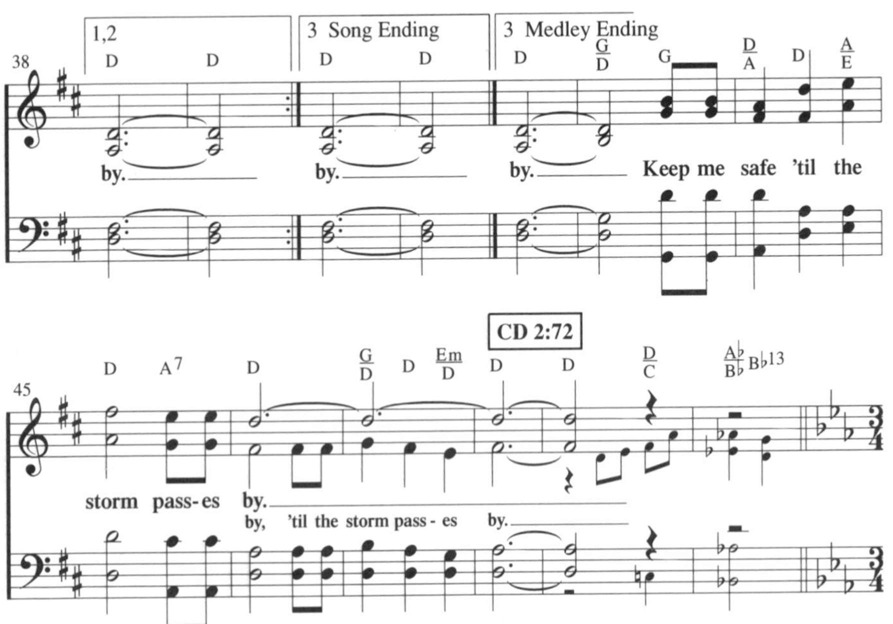

Peace in the Midst of the Storm

S.R.A.

STEPHEN R. ADAMS

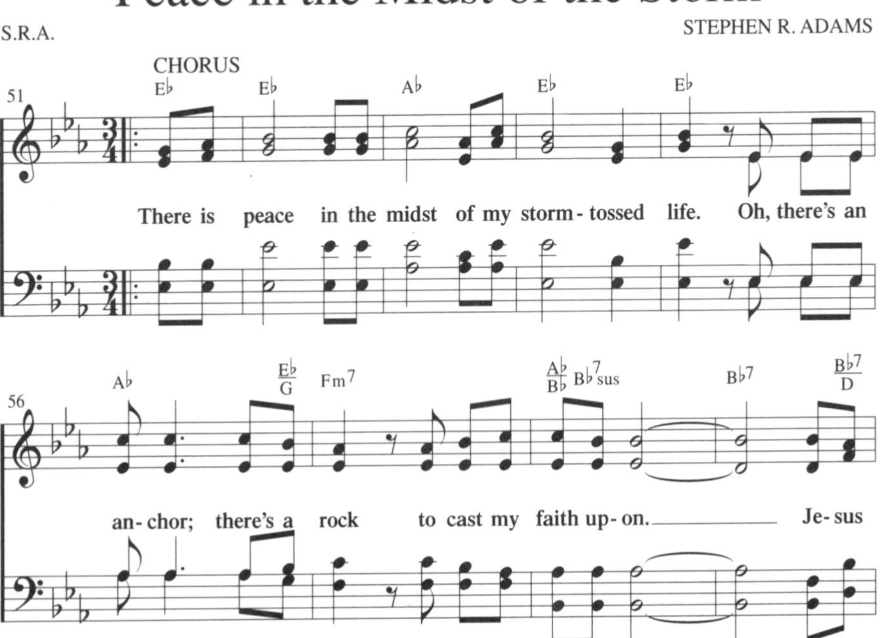

60
E♭ E♭ D♭/E♭ E♭7 A♭ A°7
rides in my ves-sel, so I'll fear no a - larm. He gives me
64
E♭/B♭ Cm6 F7/C E♭/B♭ Gm/B♭ B♭7
Medley: last time to Coda
E♭ E♭ Fine
peace in the midst of the storm.
68
E♭ B♭7sus/E♭ E♭ A♭/E♭
1. When the world that I've been liv-ing in col-
2. When in twen-ty-four short hours, years of
3. When my bod - y has been bro - ken, 'til it's
71
B♭7 A♭/B♭ B♭7 E♭ B♭/D Cm Cm7
laps-es at my feet, When my life is
liv - ing are bro't to mo - ments, And when life's fi - nal
wracked in mis - er - y, When all the doc-tors shake their
74
F9 F7 F9 Fm7/C A♭m6/C♭ B♭7 A♭/B♭ B♭7
shat-tered and torn, Tho' I'm
pic - ture is tak - ing form, In the
heads and look for - lorn, Je - sus

77
E♭
G7
G
G7
A♭6
A♭
wind-swept and bat-tered, I can cling to His
dark-room of my suf-f'ring, there's a Light comes shin-ing
comes to make my bed-side a ca-the-dral of hope and
CD 2:73
80
D♭9
E♭/B♭
B♭7
A♭/B♭
B♭7
cross And find peace in the midst of my
through; He gives me peace in the midst of my
love; He sends His peace right in-to the midst of my
1,2
3 Song Ending D.S. al Fine
3 Medley Ending
D.S. al Coda
83
E♭
E♭
E♭
E♭
E♭
E♭
storm.
storm.
storm.
storm.
CODA
89
E♭
A○7
E♭/B♭
Cm6
F7/C
E♭/B♭
B♭7
E♭
E♭
rit.
(8)
mel.
storm. He gives me peace in the midst of the storm.
End of Medley

ALPHABETICAL INDEX
Song and Medley Titles